WHAT WOMEN WISH PASTORS KNEW

Other Books by Denise George

Secrets of Soul Gardening Series

Tilling the Soul

Cultivating a Forgiving Heart

Weathering the Storms

Planting Trust, Knowing Peace

Also:

God's Heart, God's Hands: Reaching Out to Hurting Women

Teach Your Children to Pray

Our Dear Child

God's Gentle Whisper

WHAT WOMEN WISH PASTORS KNEW

UNDERSTANDING THE **HOPES, HURTS, NEEDS,** AND **DREAMS** OF **WOMEN** IN THE CHURCH

DENISE GEORGE

ZONDERVAN.com/
AUTHORTRACKER
follow your favorite authors

What Women Wish Pastors Knew
Copyright © 2007 by Denise George

Requests for information should be addressed to:

Zondervan, *Grand Rapids, Michigan 49530*

Library of Congress Cataloging-in-Publication Data

George, Denise.
 What women wish pastors knew : understanding the hopes, hurts, needs, and dreams
of women in the church / Denise George.
  p. cm.
 Includes bibliographical references.
 ISBN-13: 978-0-310-26930-4
 ISBN-10: 0-310-26930-X
 1. Women—Religious aspects—Christianity. 2. Christian women—Religious life.
3. Pastoral counseling. I. Title.
BT704.G46 2007
259.082—dc22

                   2006024640

Published in association with the literary agency of WordServe Literary Group, Ltd., 10152 S. Knoll Circle, Highlands Ranch, CO 80130.

Interior design by Mark Sheeres

Printed in the United States of America

07 08 09 10 11 12 13 • 10 9 8 7 6 5 4 3 2 1

For Dr. J. I. Packer, my longtime friend and mentor ...

with appreciation for your Christ-centered ministry,

and in celebration of your eightieth year of life!

Denise George and her son, Christian George, with Dr. Packer

CONTENTS

PASTORS DO MOST OF THEIR WORK in congregations comprised of a bewildering diversity of souls. We commonly use labels to introduce at least a modicum of order into the diversity: saints and sinners; children, elderly, and adolescents of all ages; rich, poor, and middle class; mature, immature, and neurotic; saved, unsaved, and backsliders; married, unmarried, and divorced. And men and women.

The French use an expression that I like very much, *deformation professionelle*—a liability, a tendency to defect, that is inherent in the role one has assumed as, say, a physician, a lawyer, a pastor. I have come to think that if there is a *deformation* that pastors are particularly liable to, it is our habit of presorting people into categories. Once we have a category to place them in, we have provided ourselves with a grid for dealing with them. We have reduced them by labeling them. Now we know where we stand and have a pretty good idea what we will do. The difficulty is that the label, before we even know his or her name, depersonalizes this intricately personal, one-of-a-kind, image-of-God *soul* into a some-*thing* (note, not some-*one*) that we as pastors are qualified by training and ordination to handle.

Labels have a certain usefulness if used with caution and restraint. But when used habitually and unthinkingly, stereotyping and "lumping," they are responsible for an enormous amount of damage in congregations. The damage is reciprocal: the pastor's imagination is blunted and a soul's uniqueness is violated.

The label "woman" is among the more damaging of labels used by pastors. The label depersonalizes the working identity of a large segment of any congregation into matters of gender and role. The label is then commonly subdivided into women with problems and women with gifts. If she is a problem, my job is to fix her, find a solution and get her functional. If she is a gift, my job is to put her to work, to use her as a resource. "Functional" and "resource," note, are both impersonal terms, furthering the depersonalization. The pastor is depersonalized into doing a church "job"; the woman is depersonalized into either a "problem" or "resource."

But the moment we do that, we are diverted from getting acquainted with what is most *human* in this person, *child-of-God-human*, an eternal soul with hungers and needs that are beyond our "fixing" and with gifts and abilities that cannot be slotted into a "church job." But pastors are in an enviable, and maybe even unique, position to go against the depersonalizing, functionalizing habits of our culture and recognize women as souls-in-formation, persons redefined primarily by their baptism and not by gender, their debilitating problems, or their exhilarating jobs.

Denise George is doing a wonderful thing for us pastors. She brings the voices of hundreds of women from across this land and around the world onto the pages of this book, women whose pastors haven't been listening to them. "Listen to us," they say, "you're our *pastor*!"

They, of course, have needs and gifts — don't we all? But mostly what Denise accomplishes is a massive de-labeling, a de-categorizing, letting each and every voice be heard with all the dignity inherent in every daughter of Eve, making sure that we listen, *really* listen to who they *are*, not just what they represent, or where they are slotted in a file drawer. We hear these voices making common cause with all of us as souls to be respected and honored; and are reminded that we share the demanding work of growing up to the stature of Christ.

Eugene H. Peterson
Professor Emeritus of Spiritual Theology
Regent College, Vancouver, B.C.

ACKNOWLEDGMENTS

IT HAS TAKEN A TEAM of people to put together this book! I have many to thank, including my agent, Greg Johnson, and my editor, Dr. Paul Engle. Thanks also to Zondervan's Cindy Lambert, Lyn Cryderman, Greg Clouse, and Mike Cook.

To Dr. Ed Coyne and Dr. B. Coyne, my sincerest gratitude for your knowledge, expertise, and selfless help in computerizing hundreds of survey responses. I could have never sorted through them without your help.

To the hundreds of women from all over the country who shared with me their time, thoughts, opinions, concerns, and dreams in response to my survey, thank you. I never expected such an avalanche of response!

To the faculty and staff of Beeson Divinity School who helped me collect these responses, and who encouraged me in my effort, I thank you.

To special friends who encouraged me in this project, brainstormed ideas, shared insights, and kept me in their daily prayers, I love and appreciate each of you. Thank you especially to Dr. Frank and Carolyn James, Carolyn Tomlin, Jim Cox, Jack Kuhatschek, and numerous others.

A note of appreciation to the many editors of Baptist State papers who published my survey and drew a number of responses from women across the country.

And, of course, a special thank you to my husband, Dr. Timothy George; my daughter, Alyce Elizabeth George; and my son, Christian Timothy George, and his wife, Rebecca Pounds George. You have all been great encouragers!

DEAR PASTOR (and other interested church staff, church workers, female pastors, women's ministry leaders, Sunday school teachers, pastors' wives, and church members):

Suppose you could assemble hundreds of Christian women, of all ages and stages of life, single and married, divorced and widowed — representing more than thirty denominations, almost every state in the U.S., and a few foreign countries, and every imaginable career — and ask them one specific question: "What do you wish your pastor knew?"

Would you find their candid responses valuable? Would this information help you better understand and minister to the women in your congregation?

Well, that's exactly what I did. I put the question out there (through mail and email), and I asked women to keep their names and personal information anonymous. Their responses were so many and thoughtful, I knew I had hit a nerve!

I heard from full-time homemakers and stay-at-home moms, as well as women in all areas of part-time and full-time employment — college and seminary professors, authors, teachers, businesswomen, corporate executives, secretaries, car saleswomen, nurses/health-care workers, lawyers, accountants, interior decorators, chefs, and even the driver of an eighteen-wheeler! Some emailed a sentence or two; others wrote so many pages that their surveys required extra postage!

Almost every returned survey expressed a personal note: "Finally! Thank you, Denise, for giving me this opportunity to express my heartfelt thoughts, dreams, desires, and hopes to pastors everywhere. I could never tell my pastor these things face-to-face. My prayers are with you as you write this much-needed book."

Another wrote: "Thank you for giving us a voice to our pastors' ears. I pray pastors everywhere will hear our cries."

Most of the women expressed deep love and appreciation for their pastors. They know shepherding a congregation can be tough. They also wanted to assure them of their prayers, encouragement, and support.

Some responses I expected. Other responses surprised—even shocked—me. Christian women shared their fears, temptations, insecurities, loneliness, exhaustion, pain, marriage and parenting concerns, church problems, and deep-seated opinions, in order that their pastors might better understand them, and thus better minister to them and their families.

Overwhelmed at the sheer number of responses, I immediately enlisted the graciously offered help of Dr. Ed Coyne, professor at Samford University's School of Business. Together we sorted, recorded, evaluated, and computer-analyzed the vast amount of primary data. It proved quite a task!

After "hearing" the hearts of hundreds of Christian women, I wholeheartedly agree with Dr. Rick Warren: "The church is the most magnificent concept ever created. It has survived persistent abuse, horrifying persecution, and widespread neglect. Yet despite its faults (due to our sinfulness), it is still God's chosen instrument of blessing and has been for 2,000 years."[1]

THE CHURCH'S CHALLENGE

I too value the church, as do the women who responded to the survey. That's why I think this book is so important to today's church pastors. Research shows that many churches today—God's "chosen instruments of blessing"—are suffering from declining attendance and "widespread neglect."

"People are leaving our churches by the thousands each day," writes Dr. Thom Rainer. "And others are quietly becoming less and less active."[2]

Why? One reason is the fierce competition today's church faces for the allegiance and participation of its members. The local church is no longer the center of spiritual, social, and community life. People have limitless mobility, and often fill their social/community needs at the local coffee café or sushi bar. The pull of the world in our society proves strong and often irresistible—even to devoted, "born again," evangelical Christians.

Our limited time, energy, and attention spans are drawn to extravagant shopping malls, theater multiplexes, restaurants of all ethnic persuasions, social clubs, health clubs, satellite television, sophisticated personal computer games, and a super-broadband Internet highway at our fingertips. Researchers predict that by 2010, 10 to 20 percent of the population will rely primarily or exclusively on the Internet for their religious input! They expect the "cyberchurch" to lure tens of millions of people away from the existing church.[3]

The church is also increasingly confronted and challenged by "spiritual" options—"religious" groups that pull people away. Whether paganism, witchcraft, Wicca, New Age, or goddess worship/spirituality, these pseudo-faiths are quickly "converting" our nation's women, especially our college-aged women.[4] Teenagers today experiment widely with new or rediscovered "supernatural world religions." "Three-quarters (73 percent) of America's youth have engaged in at least one type of psychic or witchcraft-related activity, beyond mere media exposure or horoscope usage."[5]

In response, local churches employ all kinds of strategies to hold onto their members and to bring the unchurched into their congregations. They build massive worship centers and equip them with theater lighting and sound technology. They design recreation centers with expensive fitness equipment, racquetball courts, bowling alleys, and swimming pools. They pad their wooden pews with "body-conforming" space-age cushions, use large-screen projectors to aid preaching, hire Hollywood celebrities and professional sports figures to give testimonies, bring in Grammy-winning recording artists to perform choreographed stage shows, host free pizza parties and elaborate church dinners, organize "skiing for Jesus" youth trips, invite older members to exotic sightseeing excursions, and even haul in super-sized televisions on Super Bowl Sunday!

But entertainment tactics don't seem to be working long term. Many lament that Sunday worship services have become Hollywood performances, producing a carnival atmosphere and a seeker-palatable, watered-down gospel. A growing number beg for serious theological, biblically based sermons and Bible study. They ask: "Isn't the Word of God powerful enough to bring people into church, and keep them there?"

"Something in me recoils," writes Dr. Charles Swindoll, "when I sense that the [worship] program is choreographed right down to the last ten seconds and I am an observer of a performance instead of a participant in worship.... When something as meaningful and beautiful as worship gets slick or bears the marks of a complicated stage show or starts to look contrived, I start checking out the closest exits."[6]

Christian women are no different.

Surely today's confused, violent, and hurting world needs the church more than ever before! Yet even with church buildings sitting on many street corners and a Bible in nearly every home and hotel room, the church's influence both within its walls and without seems to be weakening.

"Most Christian churches try to have a positive impact upon society and individuals," states George Barna. "The big question is whether what they are doing is working." He adds: "If the conclusion is that their efforts are not producing the desired outcomes, then the big challenge is whether they are willing to change their strategies to maximize their potential."[7]

BACKBONE OF THE CONGREGATION

Pastor, let me tell you something about the Christian women who sit in your church pews. They are like undiscovered gold mines that run deep beneath the foundation. While your roof leaks, your furnace smokes, and your plumbing fails to flush—while you wring your hands and worry about declining attendance, fewer volunteers, and lack of commitment—Christian women are eagerly awaiting your listening ear. Christian women hold (silently within their hearts) the solutions to many of today's ecclesiastical problems. But, they tell me, no one is listening.

Yet they have much to tell you. George Barna states that Christian women are the "backbone of the Christian congregations in America." He recently conducted a nationwide survey and published his remarkable findings, which note that, compared to men, women are:

- 100 percent more likely to be involved in discipleship;
- 57 percent more likely to participate in a small Bible study or prayer group;
- 46 percent more likely to disciple others in faith;
- 33 percent more likely to volunteer their time and help to church;
- 29 percent more likely to read the Bible;
- 29 percent more likely to share their faith with others;
- 23 percent more likely to donate to a church;
- 16 percent more likely to pray.

Barna also states there are between 11 million and 13 million more "born again" women than "born again" men in the United States. Without women, Christianity would have nearly 60 percent fewer members!

"One of the characteristics of women that emerges from the research," he writes, "is their high degree of spiritual depth.... Half of all women (49 percent) strongly desire to be personally active in a church, compared to just one-third of men (35 percent)."[8]

Barna's findings match my own. Christian women are, without a doubt, the "backbone" of today's church.

Many pastors today are asking how their church can fulfill Christ's Great Commission—"*mak[ing] disciples* of all nations, *baptizing them* in the name of the Father and of the Son and of the Holy Spirit, and *teach-*

ing them to obey everything I have commanded" (Matthew 28:18–20, my emphasis). How can their church find fresh focus, new energy, and spiritual vitality, and again become the center of true spiritual, social, and family life?

The answer is simple and profound. Enlist, teach, train, involve, and depend upon the dedicated Christian women in your church. They sit on the edge of their pews hoping for you to discover them. They are untapped treasures that eagerly wait to be unearthed, mined, and put to work for God's kingdom! Why do we allow spiritual decline in our churches when 60 percent of our congregation wants eagerly to be involved and go to work in Christ's name?

"The church will last for eternity," writes Rick Warren, "and because it is God's instrument for ministry here on earth, it is truly the *greatest force on the face of the planet....* God will give us his power to complete the task. This is God's way—ordinary people empowered by his Spirit."[9]

Ordinary Christian women, empowered by God's Spirit, can help today's church complete God's task.

Pastor, I have written this book just for you. So take off your shoes, find a comfortable chair, brew yourself a cup of strong black coffee, and read what Christian women everywhere want you to know. My prayer is that you will take their responses and use them to enrich your church for God's glory. (Note: The names and some facts have been changed to protect the privacy of the women who responded to the survey. This is an informal research project; not a scientific one.)

Let me add some personal comments here. I have a special place in my heart for today's pastor. It's a difficult job! Pastors hear a lot of criticism, and that's not the purpose of this book. Furthermore, I have been married to a minister (Timothy) for thirty-eight years. We've served both in the local church, on the home mission field, and in three seminaries. Timothy now serves as founding Dean of Beeson Divinity School at Samford University, Birmingham, Alabama. Both my grandfather, George M. Williams, and my father, Robert C. Wyse, were ministers. My twenty-four-year-old son, Christian, an MDiv student at Beeson Divinity School, is a minister-in-training. I have written two books specifically for seminary students (*How to Be a Seminary Student—And Survive* and *The Student Marriage*, both Broadman & Holman).

Denise George
Easter 2006

PART 1

THE PERSONAL
WORLD OF WOMEN
IN YOUR CHURCH

CHAPTER 1

"PASTOR, I'M TIRED"

Walk into most churches in America, have a look around, and ask yourself this question: "What is a Christian woman?" ... Don't listen to what is said, look at what you find there. There is no doubt about it. You'd have to admit, a Christian woman is ... tired.[1]

John Eldredge

WOMEN COME TO CHURCH for many reasons: They love the Lord. They want to support you, your family, and your ministry. They want to see lost people led to Christ; the sin-guilty forgiven, the sick healed, and the loveless loved. They want to work hard for God and to leave an eternal legacy for those who follow them.

But, Pastor, you should know: today's Christian woman is tired. Women listed exhaustion as their number one issue. Why do Christian women want you to know this? Do they want your sympathy? Do they want you to think they are hardworking Proverbs 31 women? Do they want to justify why they sit on back pews and run late for worship services? Do they want you to stop asking them to work in the nursery, cook church suppers, and arrange altar flowers?

The answer is no. They want you to understand that their attendance and church involvement often come at great personal sacrifice. In order to attend and work at church, a woman will often give up sleep, rest, solitude, and all personally refreshing activities—such as a walk in the woods or coffee with a friend. She will drive herself to exhaustion in order to accept the jobs you request of her.

She also wants you to know that if she declines your requests, she'll wrestle with her decision long into the night. She will take her refusal to heart, and it will usually bring her embarrassment, self-disappointment, and feelings of guilt. She might even consider herself a spiritual failure, a woman who lets her pastor down when he needs her.

Her sincere and legitimate refusals will never slide off her heart "like water off a duck's back." They'll stick like sharp briars.

Why? Because she loves you and your family. She appreciates the time, energy, and prayer you put into your ministry. You and the church are meaningful and life-giving to her and her family. She values the hard work you do. She knows how you reach out to hurting individuals in the name of Christ.

But a woman can have so many demanding responsibilities with family, home, children, career, and community, she simply does not have the physical strength to take on one more job. Even if the pastor himself personally asks her.

Most women won't tell their pastors they are tired. After all, they reason, the Proverbs 31 woman never got tired. Instead of admitting exhaustion, many women will push themselves to sickness in order to support you and the church. Other times, when exhaustion gets the best of them, they'll simply give up trying to do everything expected of them and leave the church. They figure leaving the church is less painful than declining the requests.

Women today carry heavy loads of work—at home, at their jobs, *and* at church.

George Barna sounds a "note of caution regarding the high price women may pay for carrying excessive levels of spiritual responsibility." He writes: "While women represent the lion's share of Christians and the majority of participants in religious activities, many women appear to be burning out from their intense levels of involvement." His research shows a telling "22 percent slip in church attendance [among women] since 1991," as well as a "21 percent decline in the percentage of women who volunteer to help a church."

He concludes: "Women's monumental effort to support the work of the Christian church may be running on fumes." He advises churches to "consider whether or not they are providing sufficient opportunities for women *to receive ministry* and not just *provide ministry to others*," and that "we may continue to see tens of thousands of women leaving the church unless there is a widespread, aggressive, thoughtful approach to recognizing and appreciating women."[2]

IT'S A FACT: CHRISTIAN WOMEN WON'T REST

God created the human body to need rest. Regular rest. Put your hand over your heart, and feel it beat and rest, beat and rest, beat and rest. What would happen to that life-giving muscle if it beat and beat and beat and never rested? It would burn out.

That's exactly what is happening to Christian women today. They are working hard, and they are not resting. In fact, women tell me they feel guilty when they rest. They consider hard work spiritual-ness, and rest idleness. They push themselves to exhaustion to avoid idleness.

Some women measure their level of spirituality by the amount of work they do. After all, they admit, the Proverbs 31 woman worked with eager hands, got up while it was still dark, set about her work vigorously with strong arms, and never let her lamp go out at night. She never ate the bread of idleness and surpassed all the other women with all the noble things she did.[3]

An Arkansas woman writes: "Women are overcommitted. They often tend to equate 'the busier I am' [with] 'the more spiritual I am.' They feel it is expected of them to multitask and to be leading in several different capacities. All of this overcommitment (at church, home, community, job, etc.) is a recipe for burnout, stress-out, and unhealthy and unhappy women."

THE PROVERBS 31 WOMAN AND CINDERELLA

Why do women work so hard and try to do everything so well? One reason might be that, as little girls growing up in Christian homes, many women were taught to be like two great women: the Proverbs 31 woman and Cinderella. They strive to walk in their shadows—a superwoman from Proverbs who "brings her husband praise at the city gate" and has children who call her "blessed." And a drop-dead gorgeous Cinderella who will one day "live happily ever after" with a handsome prince.

Women are taught to be beautiful, shapely, intelligent, quiet, gentle, and gracious. Society expects them to be strong and powerful, keep a husband satisfied and happy, raise up Harvard-bound kids, and find brilliant careers that bring money, fulfillment, and prestige. As *Christian* women, they are also expected to work sacrificially in church, thus doing the Lord's work to "earn their reward."

Can women today maintain spotless homes, corporate careers, happy husbands, brilliant children and, at the same time, cook like a Food Network star, decorate like Martha Stewart, look like Barbie, play tennis like Serena Williams, and evangelize like Lottie Moon? Of course not.

When, by reason of human physical limitations, they can't keep up, women often experience guilt. It's false guilt of course, but it certainly feels like the butcher knife of real guilt. So she tries to work harder—in her home, her job, her mothering, her marriage, and her church. Some women wear exhaustion like the red badge of courage. Fatigue becomes who they are—their primary identity.

BURN OUT OR RUST OUT?

"Work is fast becoming the American Christian's major source of identity," writes Charles Swindoll. "The answer to most of our problems (we are told) is 'work harder.' And to add the ultimate pressure, 'You aren't really serving the Lord unless you consistently push yourself to the point of fatigue.' It's the old burn-out-rather-than-rust-out line."[4]

Believe me, Pastor, no Christian woman wants to "rust out."

Often the church itself plays a role in a woman's guilt trip because of the expectations demanded of women in congregations.

"There is a not-so-subtle message that often equates salvation with duty to church, and women find themselves leaving hearth and home to meet these expectations that often make their lives far more difficult.... When [church roles and jobs] are mandatory and there is no flexibility, a woman can easily be overwhelmed and completely frazzled by the expectations placed upon her shoulders."[5]

Overwhelmed? Frazzled? Women used these two words a lot on their surveys. A caring pastor can teach women the difference between true guilt and false guilt. He can help them understand that while the Proverbs 31 woman can be a goal to reach for, the inexhaustible twenty-first-century Cinderella-superwoman isn't.

BIBLICAL EXAMPLES OF REST

A caring pastor can also explain to his congregation a woman's right to rest. After all, Jesus rested, even though he knew he had only three short years to accomplish his ministry on earth. And he didn't feel guilty about it. As a human being—the Word become *flesh* (John 1:14)—Jesus knew his physical limitations. To find solitude and rest, he often trekked alone into the wilderness or mountains, or sat on the grassy hills above Lake Galilee, rubbing his tired feet.

Jesus also urged his disciples to rest. The gospel writer, Mark, gives us a special insight into one chaotic event: "Then, because so many people were coming and going that they did not even have a chance to eat, [Jesus] said to them, 'Come with me by yourselves to a quiet place and get some rest.' So they went away by themselves in a boat to a solitary place" (Mark 6:31–32).

Pastor, tell the women in your church that Jesus himself offers them rest: "Come to me," he invited, "all you who labor and are heavy laden, and I will give you rest" (Matthew 11:28, NKJV).

Women need not feel guilty when they get tired—physically, mentally, emotionally, or spiritually. They must heed Jesus' call, and take the needed time to rest and replenish themselves. Quiet and solitude make for the best type of rest.

"In quiet and silence the faithful soul makes progress," writes Thomas à Kempis, "the hidden meanings of the Scriptures become clear.... As one learns to grow still, he draws closer to the Creator and farther from the hurly-burly of the world."[6]

Another prime biblical example of someone who needed rest is the great prophet Elijah. On the heels of Queen Jezebel's death threats, Scripture says: "Elijah was afraid and ran for his life" (1 Kings 19:3). Exhausted and seized by terror, Elijah traveled alone to the desert. He prayed a defeated prayer, and asked God to let him die. "I have had enough, Lord," he cried. "I'm totally stressed out and ready to throw in the towel" (19:4, my paraphrase).

What did God do? He made Elijah rest. Elijah lay down under a broom tree and slept. God's angel woke him with bread and water, and then he went back to sleep and rested again. God's prescription worked. So strengthened by rest and solitude and nourishment, Elijah got up and "traveled forty days and forty nights until he reached Horeb" (19:4–8). You see, God had a job for Elijah. He had an important message to give him. God knew Elijah must be rested in order to climb a mountain and accurately hear God's "gentle whisper" (19:12).

Believe me, Pastor, that'll preach to the women in your church![7]

MEET YOUR CHURCH MEMBER, "SISTER SALLY"

Allow me to introduce you to the "Sallys" in your congregation. They are numerous, and they are tired. Let's become a fly on Sally's kitchen wall on an average Sunday morning, as she prepares herself and her family for Sunday school and church worship.

Sally just turned thirty-four. The mother of three girls—ages seven, four, and two months—she works full time outside the home, as does her husband. Together they are trying to pay off some high medical bills, as well as keep a roof over their children's heads and food on their table. Sally's widowed mother, in ailing health, also lives with the family.

Do you see Sally in her robe standing at the stove scrambling eggs? She spent yesterday cleaning, washing clothes, grocery shopping, preparing meals, and bathing her daughters. She collapsed into bed long after midnight—exhausted. Before she turned out the light, she noticed her husband's winking eye and the telltale grin on his face.

This morning her alarm clock rang at 6:00 a.m. She jumped out of bed, laid out the children's church clothes, woke her mother and husband, and is now getting ready to feed them breakfast. Then she'll clean the kitchen, organize Sunday lunch, dress the children, diaper and nurse the baby, and slip into her own church clothes.

Now begins the race to church. Sally gathers up Bibles and offering envelopes, herds her children out the door, buckles them into the family van, and urges her mother and husband to hurry.

Sally's husband isn't enthusiastic about going to church since Sunday is his only morning to sleep late. He yawns and grumbles on the way. When they arrive at church, they drop off her mother by the main door, hunt for a parking place, and then rush into the building. Sally helps her mom to the seniors class, sees the girls to Sunday school and the nursery respectively, then meets up with her husband at the young parents class. She has already walked—in dress heels—the equivalent of five city blocks. And it's only 9:00 a.m.

After the Sunday school hour, Sally rounds up her children and finds the rest of the family in the sanctuary. Then she slips out, finds a ladies' room, and nurses the baby. She arrives back and sits down just as an enthusiastic song leader asks her to stand. Baby over one shoulder, she sings multiple verses of the new praise chorus. Sally will sit and stand at least six more times before you preach.

After your sermon, she'll meet and greet fellow worshipers, then meander with her husband, mother, and kids back to the van. Everyone is starving, the older girls are elbow-jabbing each other in the back seat, and the baby, now crying, smells bad. They arrive home, unload the van, and Sally kicks off her shoes, changes the baby, and serves lunch. Then she cleans the kitchen, and gets an hour to herself if she's lucky. If the church holds an evening service, Sally will jump up and start all over again. Before Sally goes to bed late that night, she will organize her girls' things for school and day care, pack lunches, and press her business suit.

And that's on a *good* Sunday—when the van will start, the storm has stopped, and the girls don't have diarrhea, flu, or chicken pox!

Believe it or not, this is the typical Sunday morning workload required by many of your congregation's wives and mothers in order to attend Sunday school and worship services. (And you thought preparing a sermon was exhausting!)

If Sally doesn't slow down, take time to rest, and allow God to refill her empty spiritual pitcher—through quiet, prayer, and solitude, Sally will wrestle with increasing exhaustion, and may very well surrender to her husband's preference to sleep in on Sunday.

If you want to keep stressed-out Sister Sally in church, teach her not only to physically rest but provide her with a Sunday worship experience that both quiets and energizes her soul.

WOMEN AND STRESS

Sally isn't the only Christian woman today who deals with stress.

An Alabama woman writes: "There is a huge strain on women today. We are balancing careers/children/church and so much more. Many of us struggle with getting to church, and we often have no help from our spouse. I see so many women (especially young mothers) 'limping' to church, so worn down and defeated and overwhelmed. They need encouragement."

An Illinois woman agrees: "Women need balance in their lives. We try to balance home and work, and feel a constant conflict between them. We spend our breaks at work calling for doctors' appointments, etc. After a full day of work, we come home to another full day of work. Women still carry the burden of most housework. We feel guilty for leaving our children in someone else's care. We need time to spend with our husbands, and we need time to be alone. We want to work in our church. We need time to spend with God."

A woman from Arkansas responds: "I am a thirty-seven-year-old married woman with two children, ages three and five. I wish my pastor knew how tired I am! I am a wife, mother, student, and the caretaker of my elderly father. I am to be sexually available to my husband. And then, I am to volunteer for Awana, teach Sunday school, do nursery duty, and provide food for the staff luncheons. I don't have time to do any Bible study. I am told to be like Mary, who sat at Jesus' feet while Martha worried. But if I sit at Jesus' feet, I will fall asleep. Christian women are asked to do the impossible."

A California woman writes: "Women are stressed about trying to do it all and be it all. Especially those of us in church! We want our kids to turn out right, our husbands to be wonderfully happy, and we want to do everything the church asks us. Trying to find a balance and not feel guilty is very hard. Trying to be super [church] workers and supermoms is taking its toll on us. We are tired—burnt out, and forced by societal definitions to keep working."

A Nebraska woman writes: "I feel so overwhelmed! Surely, God never intended for women to wear so many hats, but yet here I am, wearing them all. Make the world stop spinning. I want to get off."

A Kansas woman agrees: "Women are really, really tired! We have too much to do, too many demands on us, and not enough sleep! We just can't balance it all. Many women are forced to work outside the home, and carry large financial responsibilities. When we return home from work, we are tired, but we still have mother/wife/church roles to fulfill. I don't get time to take a deep breath, enjoy a hobby, read a book, go for a walk, talk to a friend, etc. Every minute of my day is taken."

"The stress load on the working mother is titanic," claims writer Betty Cuniberti. "Among ... working mothers, tales abound of guilt; of the inability to juggle the demands of work, children, a husband and a home without being fatigued and feeling inadequate."[8]

THE PROBLEM OF FALSE GUILT

False guilt follows many women like hungry puppies. They retire at night and awake at daybreak with guilt-causing questions attacking their minds:

- *As a wife:* Am I giving my husband the time he needs? Am I satisfying him sexually? Do I keep our home clean enough, organized enough? Am I supporting him adequately in his career?
- *As a mother:* Do I spend enough quality time with my children? Am I raising them to be spiritually minded adults? Am I meeting their health needs regarding food and diet, and doctor's checkups? Am I giving them the educational opportunities they need? Am I creating a good home atmosphere for them? Am I showing them enough love and care and concern?
- *As a daughter of aging parents:* Am I meeting their health needs? Am I spending enough time with them? Do I need to help them more financially?

- *As an employed woman:* Am I carrying my load at work? Do I depend on other workers too much? Do I miss too many work days due to personal or family sickness? Do I have a healthy balance between work and family responsibilities?
- *As a church woman:* Am I adequately supporting my pastor and church with my prayers? Am I giving enough money to the church? Should I be more involved with church programs? Should I be teaching a Sunday school class or working with the church's children? Why can't I go to church every time I am requested to be there?

Such guilt-wracking questions also include a woman's responsibilities to friends, neighbors, children's teachers, charities, worthwhile community projects, and so on.

A WOMAN'S LACK OF QUIET TIME WITH GOD

Another common complaint among women is lack of time to spend with God in Bible study, prayer, and meditation. A Christian woman's relationship with God is paramount in her life. In order to meet the demands of family, home, work, and church, she needs the inner strength that only regular quiet time gives her. If excess work and overcommitment eat away her personal worship time, her whole being will get out of sorts. Everything else in her life will be affected in a negative way.

A Tennessee mother writes: "The average woman today must be a Christian mother to school-aged children, a wife, work a full-time job, and attend church activities. It's hard for her to find daily, personal meditation time and prayer. This is essential to keep her spiritual life in perspective."

A woman from Indiana acknowledges: "I'm tired! I work outside the home, and all the things I do pull me in fourteen different directions at once. Even though I want to put God first, sometimes he gets put on the 'back burner.'"

From Alabama: "I believe church women are so busy in their lives and church, their relationship with God gets lost in the shuffle. They are encouraged to serve, but not to grow spiritually."

And from Georgia: "Exhaustion has got to be one of the most looming problems for moms and working women. We are so tired, we rarely have quiet time, devotions, and prayer; just where Satan wants us ... diffused."

WHAT CAN PASTORS DO TO HELP TIRED WOMEN?

Pastor, you can help the tired woman in your congregation by showing her how to:

1. *Prioritize her workload and activities, and seek God's guidance (through Bible study, prayer, and/or counseling), before committing to too many work responsibilities.*

A woman from Minnesota writes: "The number one problem for Christian women is balance. I think we need help learning to stay centered in Christ."

A West Virginia woman agrees: "A woman needs to be spiritually fed by her church, and then *be very selective* about what she commits to do."

2. *Say no gracefully but firmly, and seek to establish a workable life balance.*

An Idaho mother writes: "As a mom, time is precious and I can't always keep up with family and church. I want my pastor/church to teach me to balance my church and home responsibilities."

A Texas woman admits: "I often struggle with weariness. I believe women need to be told it's okay to say no. They should only commit to what they know God is calling them to do. Overcommitment at church only leads to weary women (especially if they work outside the home), making them easy targets for Satan and his attacks. And this has a snowball effect on marriage and families. Is it possible that an emphasis on setting godly priorities for women—teaching women how to say no—could help women in their daily decisions and thus combat this weariness? I believe it could!"

"Just because I do not serve on a committee or in other capacities every time I am asked," states a Tennessee woman, "does not mean I am indifferent to church needs. It means I am older, wiser, and more able to discern God's will for my life. Believe me, I don't get it right every time, but I do know where my strengths lie. I don't want others to criticize me because I am not doing VBS [Vacation Bible School] or WMU [Woman's Missionary Union] work regularly, or because my children aren't there every time the church door is open. A woman today must learn to 'number her days'!"

Pastors greatly help church women when they take the time, energy, and forethought to teach them how to depend on God's guidance in choosing work and activities; how to create a balanced life by prioritizing job, home, and church responsibilities; and how to feel guiltless when they must honestly decline an additional job. Pastors can help women learn to say no with kindness and grace, but also with nonnegotiable firmness.

Pastors can help women in other ways too. For instance, a pastor can:

1. *Watch (and ask others in the church to watch) for overworked and exhausted women in the congregation, and then minister specifically to them.*

A career woman from Ohio writes: "Sometimes even though we, as women, say we are doing well, we really aren't. Today many women work outside the home, then come home to fix meals, wash clothes, etc. Some tend to get overwhelmed and just need a time-out. The pastor might ask his wife or another staff member to look out for such women. That would create a more loving and caring relationship between the pastor and the congregation. There was a time several years ago that I myself would have been the one who needed a time-out."

2. *Realize and affirm a woman's daily existing ministry—outside the church walls.*

An Illinois woman writes: "Pastor, please know that most Christian women want to be used by the church. I think most women feel they already "do" ministry—by touching lives every day when they care for their families; when they minister to people at their jobs, and in their neighborhood and community, and when they take over other jobs at home so their husbands can take leadership roles at church."

Another woman writes: "Just because a woman may not be involved in a 'formal' ministry of the church doesn't mean she doesn't have a ministry. For instance, my friend had a meeting with our former pastor. He told her that she 'hadn't done anything for ten years.' (By 'anything,' he meant being involved in a 'formal ministry' of our church.) During those years, my friend's mother suffered from Alzheimer's disease. My friend spent a lot of time with her mother, and tried to help her father deal with his wife's devastating illness. My friend also worked full-time as a nurse (because her husband wanted her to work). She had one teenager still at home, and was involved in the lives of her two older, married children, as well as her grandchildren. Several times she opened up her home for bridal or baby showers for friends in the church. (That was certainly a ministry to the families involved!) I think there are times in a woman's life when God calls her to things that maybe aren't 'official ministries,' but they are important to him. I can think of another friend who is also a nurse with a busy schedule. For years, she has opened her home for church functions. She often invites people over for lunch after church services. She also makes herself available to those in our church who are sick in the hospital or dying. To me, that is what 'body life' is all about—even though her name isn't written down on some roster!"

3. *Distribute the church's workload more evenly and equally among the women.*

"Some pastors have new ministries they want their church to do," writes an Oklahoma woman. "That is good. But today's moms are sometimes stretched to their limit—and beyond—and can't take on additional ministries. We have to involve more people, which is difficult to do in small churches, or we need to allow people to rotate through these ministries."

4. *Resist the temptation to question a church woman's reasons for declining your church-work requests, and thus keep her from experiencing the common "guilt trip syndrome."*

"Women in the church often need permission or encouragement from the pastor to guard their time," acknowledges a Tennessee woman. "Church work comes third in our priorities (we are to first be in a love relationship with God; second to be in relationship with those God put in our lives; and third, to do the work of his creation). We must carefully allocate our scarce resource of time. Obviously, this is an area of personal struggle. Moms, whether professionals like myself or the stereotypical soccer moms of the twenty-first century, balance many things—church work included. Guilt is a very common feeling among many I know."

5. *Consider/research/understand/appreciate a woman's age and stage of life, as well as her special life circumstances before you ask her to do church work.*

Stacy Wiebe explains: "Too much doing, going, helping and giving can take a toll on [women], physically, emotionally and spiritually. Most medical books attribute anywhere from 50 to 80 percent of all diseases to stress-related origins. When I get really busy, I'm quick to cut corners on the Big Three: sleep, exercise and healthy eating. Too much busyness also chafes at the soul. Irritability, frustration, anger, bitterness, burnout and even depression can result. In seeking to serve others, [we women] often neglect our own needs and run out of inner resources from which to draw strength. Spiritually, we become starved.... Busyness inevitably affects our relationships. We often don't have energy or time to invest with friends and family. Activity can become a substitute for intimacy."[9]

An Alabama woman agrees: "There are too many church programs and commitments we're asked to give our time and effort to. We don't have time to be in relationship with others because we're stretched too thin and we're too busy 'doing.'"

Another writes: "Women, even when not employed outside their home, are often still wives, mothers, cooks, cleaners, etc. at home. Be careful not to overload even the most incredibly able and willing ones."

6. *Be mindful and considerate of a woman's time during church programs, extra scheduled events, and committee meetings.*

A South Carolina woman complains: "Being asked to attend endless meetings is simply not a priority for most of us. However, not being at every meeting may mean that we are shut out of opportunities to serve in areas where some of us could make valid contributions."

Another admits: "It is not easy for women to go to each event the church sponsors. Pastors must understand that sometimes women can be really tired. After the event, let them go home ASAP. Because sometimes the event just keeps going on and on … like forever."

Most women today would agree with Henri Nouwen when he states: "Our lives often seem like over-packed suitcases bursting at the seams. In fact, we are almost always aware of being behind schedule."[10]

For the sake of busy women, wives, and mothers, be diligent to begin and end church events/meetings at an agreed-upon time. Consider a woman's schedule before you plan an event that will involve her participation. Take a careful look at your church's schedule and ask:

- Why do we meet as a church when we do? Could we consider changing our scheduled worship/meeting times to coordinate better with the congregation's schedule?
- Are our meeting times scheduled so that busy women (and families) can more easily attend them? Do they end at a promised time so that families can have the adequate sleep and preparation time required to get up the next morning, dress for school and jobs?
- Are we combining some of our church events to happen when women, and their families, are already at the church?
- Could we provide mothers with appropriate child care when we ask them to participate in Bible studies, church-sponsored events, women's ministry activities, etc.?
- Could we provide simple family meals after church services/activities to help young mothers with small children (or grandmothers raising grandchildren full-time), and thus reduce their stressful rush (and extra workload) to get home and prepare a meal?

7. *Seek ways to provide rest and refreshment for your church women, and teach them to rest.*

"Overcommitted women need spiritual food for wisdom," confesses a Texas woman. "They need extra rest for physical strength and energy, as well as a double dose of that medicine that doeth good — laughter.

Pastor, please start a women's ministry program in our church that can help our women deal with these problems! Without a godly, organized women's ministry, or a spirit-led mentoring program, women will tend to risk taking on too much, resent what they do for the church, and eventually just burn out!"

"I'd like to see our church's women's ministry team provide more opportunities for women to retreat and rest," agrees a Virginia woman. "And when we get to a quiet retreat place, please don't fill it full of workshops and worship services and sing-a-longs and small group discussions that will eat up all our rest time."

An Alabama woman writes: "It would benefit the church greatly if the pastor would put an 'emphasis on women' and their need to take time away to relax, regroup, and just have fun. Most pastors and church staff aren't very sensitive to the special need for women to have time off from their children. Pastors could also encourage their husbands (if they are married) to stay home and keep the children, help around the house, and give 'Mama' some time off."

"It doesn't require a Ph.D. from Princeton to assess that we are busy, busy, busy. Forever on the move, doing things, eating stuff, working, jumping, jogging, writing, marrying, divorcing, buying ... you name it, our country is doing it.... The pace is somewhere between maddening and insane. The freeways are shocked with traffic, people are going and coming twenty-four hours every day ... with no letup in sight. Faces reflect tension. The air is polluted. The earth shakes. The malls are crowded. Nerves are shot."[11]

As a pastor, you have the perfect opportunity to teach the women in your church how to escape from the "maddening and insane" pace, and take needed time to rest. Give them permission to stop work, take off their shoes, and prop up their feet! Through your words, your personal example, and your encouragement, women will learn to rest. And the kingdom of God—as well as your church—will be better for it.

Today's Christian woman wants her pastor to know that:

- She is tired. Stress, overwork, and too many responsibilities for home, family, career, and church are causing extreme exhaustion—physically, emotionally, mentally, and spiritually. In light of those demands, her church attendance and volunteerism are inevitably slipping.
- When she can't keep up with this overwhelming workload, she feels incredible guilt. She will overwork herself to the point of burnout in order to avoid feeling guilty.
- She wants to spend more personal quiet time with God in Scripture study, meditation, and prayer. But she is frustrated because, in light of her busy schedule and the necessary demands of others, she simply doesn't have time for these spiritual disciplines.
- Just because she can't do more work at church—due to her all-consuming schedule—she is not "unspiritual" and "unwilling" and "unsupportive" of the pastor and church. A greater amount of church work does not equal a greater amount of personal spirituality.
- Ministry also happens outside the church walls, and she "ministers" constantly to others.
- Due to her exhaustion and demanding schedule, she might have to decline your request to volunteer in the church. Never take her refusal personally.
- More evenly distributed work among the church's women will mean that no one woman will be burdened with too heavy a load.
- She needs you and the church (through Scripture's teachings) to give her permission to rest.
- She needs you and the church to help her learn how to rest, how to better prioritize her time/activities, and how to bring more balance to her life.

CHAPTER 2

"PASTOR, I HURT"

It ... seems as if our society were designed to break the human spirit. Rather than a style of life, it might be called a style of death.[1]

Arthur Gish

IN THE PREVIOUS CHAPTER, we saw how women today are overworked, overwhelmed, and just plain tired. Let me clarify what we mean by "tired." There are two kinds of "tired." One is "good tired," the tired we feel after we do a job well, or accomplish a difficult task. Our body, mind, and emotions may feel exhausted, but after some Elijah-like food and rest, we recover and regain our strength and positive outlook on life.

The other tired is "dangerous tired." "This condition is deeper and more serious than the temporary exhaustion that follows times of periodic intensity in our schedules and workloads.... Dangerous tired is an atmospheric condition of the soul that is volatile and portends the risk of great destruction. It is a chronic inner fatigue."[2]

DANGEROUS TIRED

"Dangerous tired" happens when a woman is continually overworked and overstressed in her daily life. Little daily stresses accumulate—one on top of another, until they overwhelm a woman with exhaustion—a "chronic inner fatigue."

Karl Menninger writes: "The repetition of minor irritations and frustrations may be cumulative in their effects to a disturbing degree."[3] If these little daily stresses continue to accumulate without resolution, and if the average woman's Herculean workload doesn't ease up, she will get sick.

One person "reacts to increased tension with a headache, another with high blood pressure, and still another with sleeplessness, irritability, and depression."[4] The end result of overwork and unresolved, accumulated, daily stress is usually disturbing discomfort and certain dis-ease.

"Clearly, something is out of balance," John Talbot and Steve Rabey write, "when millions of people are wracked by stress and medicated against despair. Not that life is a picnic. Hardly. Daily living can be full of challenge and pain."[5]

Some women live their entire lives with inner fatigue. They've never learned that women can live any other way. They learned the "style of death" from their grandmothers and mothers who worked too hard and died too young. They depend on strong black coffee for alertness, sugary foods for instant energy, ibuprofen to ease body aches, and tranquilizers to stabilize their despair, impatience, and irritability. They race to and fro, always run behind schedule, keep a cell phone glued to their ear, and growl at their watch like it's a clawing kitty.

The late Paul Brand, noted medical doctor and author, wrote: "When we are under severe strain, maybe resulting from an accumulation of small stresses—bills, work pressures, irritating habits of family members—suddenly every minor frustration hits like a blow. We have become hypersensitive, and our minds are telling us we need a respite as surely as neuronal hypersensitivity warns our bodies of a need for relief."[6]

Author Susan Forward agrees: "When we don't protect our bodies, they signal us with pain until we pay attention.... I certainly don't go along with the idea that every physical ailment is psychosomatic, but there is ample evidence that the mind, emotions and body are intimately connected. Emotional distress can significantly increase our vulnerability to headaches, muscle spasms, gastrointestinal problems, respiratory disorders and a host of other ailments."[7]

Pastor, many of the women in your church are hurting. They hurt from dangerous tiredness and severe strain. Not only does the accumulated stress in their lives make them sick, but some face traumatic and intense situations they can't cope with or control. Some suffer deep pain, and some experience crises that can emotionally and physically cripple them. And so much of the time, they suffer in silence.

MEET SOME OF YOUR "SILENT" CHURCH WOMEN

Let me take you deep into the lives and secrets of some of the hurting women in your congregation. Sunday after Sunday they listen to you preach and nod in agreement with your three main sermon points. They might look spit-polished on the outside—decked out in stylish clothes, shoes, and accessories. They might even force a wide, toothy smile. But inside, their broken hearts tell a much different story.

Meet Marva

Marva, thirty-five, is attractive and outgoing. But just behind that vivacious smile, Marva is aching. She and her husband are infertile. They have tried for a dozen years to conceive. They've been to gynecologists and internists and fertility clinics, and have spent a fortune on possible "cures." They have searched the Scriptures for answers and prayed earnestly for a child. But God seems silent. Marva is faithful to the church, and she never misses a single service or activity—except for Mother's Day and baby-dedication Sunday. She just can't bear to watch the usual parade of joyful moms, proud dads, and bouncy babies.

Pastor, according to national statistics, Marva is likely not alone among your congregation. According to national statistics, more than 5.3 million Americans of reproductive age deal with infertility, or about one in forty-four.[8]

An infertile woman from Mississippi writes: "While pastors are preaching to families and about families ... there are many that may desperately want children ... whose hearts are breaking. I was never bitter at those who were pregnant, but it was hard not to feel overlooked in the heartbreak that came with waiting for God's time."

Meet Kayla

Last year, Kayla's twenty-three-year-old daughter, Marie, killed herself, leaving behind two small children. Kayla, fifty, now has the job of raising her granddaughters. Kayla has no living parents and/or siblings to help her. Her husband left her years ago. She feels quite alone in her pain. Kayla yearns for someone in the church to reach out to her, and to help her deal with her daughter's suicide. And the women in the church want to help, but they feel awkward. They don't know what to say or do. They are hesitant to even make eye contact with Kayla. Meanwhile Kayla suffers alone and falls to sleep at night blaming herself for Marie's death: "Could I have done something to prevent it? Did I raise her wrong? Did I love her enough? Did she know how much I loved her?"

There's no way to predict how many women in your congregation will commit suicide, or lose a husband or child or parent to suicide. But, no doubt, you'll face it again. Each year, suicide accounts for about 29,000 deaths in the United States. Suicide claims more American lives than homicide (about 19,000) or AIDS (about 13,000). And suicide rates are increasing. More than half a million people attempt suicide every year, but fail to complete it. Young people, like Marie, are at a high risk for suicide. Suicide is the third-leading cause of death among fifteen- to twenty-four-year-olds.[9]

Meet Cindy and Her Daughter, Lisa

Cindy has been a devoted single mother to her seventeen-year-old daughter, Lisa. Church worship and attendance have been a major focus in their lives, and Lisa has been a "regular" at choir, youth activities, and mission events. Two weeks ago, however, Cindy was shocked when she discovered Lisa was sexually active and three months pregnant. The seventeen-year-old "boy-father" is no longer interested. Both Cindy and Lisa will need your urgent counsel as they make tough decisions about what to do next.

Lisa isn't the only young woman in your congregation who is sexually active. Most young people begin having sex in their mid-to-late teens, about eight years before they marry. In fact, more than half of the seventeen-year-olds in your church have had intercourse. Teens are less likely than older women to practice contraception, and each year, almost a million teenage girls (10 percent of all women aged fifteen to nineteen and 19 percent of those who have had sexual intercourse) become pregnant. Some 13 percent of all U.S. births are to teens, and 78 percent of those births to teens outside of marriage. One-fourth of the unmarried teen-aged mothers in your church will have a second child within two years of their first! Some of the pregnancies you will know about through word of mouth or because they produce a baby. But nearly four out of every ten teen pregnancies in your church (excluding those ending in miscarriages) will be terminated by abortion.[10]

If Lisa carries her baby full term, gives birth, and decides to keep her child, she will become one of the nation's many single moms. The challenge for the church will be to minister to her and her infant, and resist judging her because of her premarital sexual conduct.

A young woman from Alabama writes: "Although I haven't had personal experience with this, I have talked with women who are single mothers — those who have had children out of wedlock. Unfortunately, this problem has become more and more common in our society. But even more unfortunate is how some churches handle these situations. I believe that, just like in *The Scarlet Letter* [the literary classic about a young woman scorned for committing adultery], we all make mistakes. But unmarried moms have an obvious and lasting reminder of their mistake, whereas many of us can hide our wrongdoings from the world. These single moms often feel judged by the church. That harsh judgment ultimately turns them away from God, when instead the church should be seeking to bring them closer to God!"

Meet Margaret

Two years ago, Margaret, thirty-five, and the mother of one, became pregnant. Her husband, Jack, didn't want another baby, so he strongly urged an abortion. After much emotional struggle and many sleepless nights, Margaret finally agreed to the procedure. But she has not been the same since, suffering serious problems with guilt, anger, anxiety, depression, and even thoughts of suicide.[11] Her marriage isn't doing so well either.

Members of Margaret's Sunday school class noticed the sudden change in her, but didn't want to pry into her personal business. Though she yearned to confess the abortion and seek counseling through the church, she feared rejection. She has dropped out of Sunday school and church, and ignores all invitations to come back.

Margaret suffers from abortion-caused guilt, commonly called post-abortion syndrome.[12] And she's not alone. Based on statistics, forty-three women in one hundred, under the age of forty-five, already have had, or will have, at least one abortion! Twenty-one of them will deal with abortion-caused guilt, and at least half of those will regret having the abortion.[13]

The women in your church will have abortions for various reasons. Some will want to postpone childbearing — it just isn't convenient — or they might think they are too young to become a mother. Some can't afford a baby. Others, like Margaret, have a partner or husband who doesn't want a child — or another child. Still others fear a child will disrupt a career and/or education. Only a fraction of women today have an abortion due to risky fetal and/or maternal health.

Meet Lela

Lela, forty-five, has just become the full-time caretaker for her mother, who suffers from Alzheimer's disease. Lela is single, and the only sibling—out of two brothers and two sisters—who has volunteered care. Lela has quit the career she loves. She's sold her home and moved in with her mother. She hates the disease that has disrupted her and her mother's lives.

Alzheimer's creates problems for two types of women in your church: the disease's victim and the victim's caretaker. Alzheimer's will affect one in ten people over age sixty-five in your congregation, and nearly half of your members over age eighty-five. By 2050, if a cure or preventive measure isn't found in the meantime, the number of Americans with Alzheimer's will increase from four million to fourteen million![14]

Alzheimer's is not the only reason an elderly person needs a full-time caretaker. According to the U.S. Census Bureau, more than one-third of adults aged sixty-five years or older have a disability that can be classified as severe, and more than 16 percent require basic nursing or assistance with daily activities. This degree of impairment is present in more than half of those aged eighty years and older, with more than one-third needing assistance with personal care or chronic health conditions. With the number of elderly people increasing each year, more and more women will be called on to take care of aging parents.

Who are the women in your church who will most likely assume full- or part-time caretaking responsibilities for diseased and/or elderly parents? The typical caregiver is a woman family member, who is married, works full-time outside her home, and is in her mid forties.[15] She might also have teenagers, grown children, and even grandchildren. Not only will she be required to divide her limited time between job and family, but she must also share it with caretaking tasks. Her time to work in the church, or attend church activities, will be limited as well.

Meet Elaine

A forty-year-old married woman with teenagers, Elaine lives daily with the memories of her father's decade-long sexual abuse. In the past, Elaine suffered bouts of alcohol abuse and eating disorders, and even now she regularly struggles with a poor body image, low self-esteem, deep depression, and suicidal thoughts. Elaine and her husband have sexual and marital problems. If she doesn't get help, her marriage will probably end in divorce.

Elaine believes in God and regularly attends church. But she doesn't believe God loves her or that he is kind and patient. Elaine thinks God is like her father, so she fears him, and when she prays, she never expects him to answer.[16]

Elaine's tragic childhood has left her with severe insecurities in many areas of her life. She desperately wants to be free from the past's pain, but can't escape it.[17]

A Tennessee woman writes: "There are far too many hurting women in their congregations who are bound by things in their past. They cannot operate in full capacity with this bondage. Women want to be taught how to be set free from this 'excess baggage' and operate fully in their God-given gifts."

A South Carolina woman agrees: "Many women in the church today put on the *show* of a Christian woman, but inside they are hurting and void. They crave some kind of reassurance that God hears their prayers. For me, especially, I struggle with holding on to my faith when my prayers seemingly go unanswered. I want to do God's will, but somehow that gets clouded by the frustrations of my present condition, and I feel lost ... stuck in this place that I'm not really sure how I got to, and am definitely not sure of how I'm going to get out of. I don't know what to do."

Pastor, at least twenty to twenty-five women in a congregation of a hundred women have suffered sexual abuse as a girl! In a majority of cases, the abuse comes from a girl's father or another trusted family member.[18, 19]

Few Christian women will talk about it. They are embarrassed and ashamed. They may keep their secret for a lifetime. Current data indicates that all forms of child sexual abuse against females in the United States are rampant. Studies reveal that from 27 percent to 54 percent of all females have experienced some form of child sexual abuse. "It is estimated that there are thirty-four million adult women in our country today who were molested as children."[20, 21]

Meet Kathy

A bright, single college student, Kathy, twenty-two, loves Jesus and is active in her church. Recently, however, she has had some worries about her sexuality. Two weeks ago, she felt "inappropriate sexual feelings" for a woman in her small group. She is ashamed, embarrassed, and doesn't know how to handle these feelings. She wonders if she might be a lesbian and is disgusted by the thought. She wants to discuss it with someone in the church, but worries about what they might think of her.

Surprisingly, a number of the survey responses confess concerns about homosexuality.

A young woman from Mississippi writes: "I know women in my church who struggle with lesbianism just as often as men struggle with homosexuality. These women put on a happy face and cover up so many issues in their lives.... Surely it is much easier to deal with things—like feelings of lesbianism—knowing that someone else has gone through similar issues, and is still pressing on."

Another writes: "Women long for spiritual wholeness—they yearn to fill and mend the voids in their hearts. It's hard to talk to a pastor about such issues ... especially if that pastor is a man."

Meet Mary

Mary is seventy and her husband of forty years died nine months ago. Shy and with few friends, she lives alone. Her grown children live a distance from her and rarely visit. Mary is one of ten million widows in the United States today, and one of the 175,000 women who become new widows each year.[22] Mary won't ask the church for help, but she is sad, grief-stricken, and overcome with loneliness. The first year of widowhood has been especially hard for her. She wonders sometimes if she wants to live.[23]

A large number of surveyed church widows admit they are intensely lonely and don't know where to turn for help.

A Texas widow writes: "I wish my pastor knew the loneliness and emptiness I feel. I feel pain and suffering, and I have constant suicidal thoughts."

A widow from Florida admits: "I feel so alone in the church since my husband died, and I am no longer 'a couple.'"

A West Virginia widow suggests: "I would like to see the younger women or couples adopt a widow or widower. Take us to lunch, shopping, the post office, and on other errands. Some of us are so lonely, and it would do much to cheer us up and make us feel special. We often need transportation and volunteers to help us get to church."

Pastor, I've introduced you to just a handful of the hurting women who sit in your church pews and suffer in silence. They need not suffer alone, however. In the next chapter, we'll look at some ways you and the church can help them.[24]

Today's Christian woman wants her pastor to know that:

- She hurts—physically, emotionally, mentally, and spiritually.
- Her schedule is dangerously overloaded, and the accumulated and constant daily stress is making her ill.
- Christian women today often live in a frazzled state of "dis-ease."
- Women often face tremendous societal obstacles, deep relational challenges, overwhelming personal struggles, and unexpected painful crises. They need help, relief, healing, and spiritual direction from their pastor and church.
- Women want their pastors to look deeper into their lives and struggles, and to understand the ways in which they often suffer.

PART 2

THE FAITH
OF WOMEN IN
YOUR CHURCH

CHAPTER 3

"PASTOR, I NEED BIBLICAL COUNSELING"

> *The very structure of our brains is dramatically impacted by adverse experiences.... The pain we try to suppress or repress doesn't just go away; unless these experiences are acknowledged, expressed, and resolved, emotional pressure continues to build, producing suffering and distress.*[1]
>
> **Harold Bloomfield**

WOMEN APPRECIATE a pastor's counseling.

A woman from Louisiana writes: "My pastor is wonderful and gentle to hurting women in our church. When my husband of twenty-five years just up and left, my pastor was careful to bring his wife over to my home, and pray often with me. My pastor called me forward during one Sunday morning worship service, and he had those in the congregation who knew me come forward and pray with me. He prayed a 'prayer covering of protection' over me. He prayed that I would see God's hand holding me up until the trouble cleared. Little did my pastor know how much this meant. I pray more church pastors will pray with other women who go through the pain of divorce. It's not unusual for pastors to pray with and for church widows. But divorced women can be often 'set aside' and ignored. My pastor helped me feel lifted up when I felt 'damaged' and tossed in the 'discontinued bin.'"

A woman from Alabama writes: "I am blessed with a pastor and support staff that do a very commendable job of communicating both biblical truth *and* true compassion to the women of our congregation."

Another, from Arkansas, writes: "I think I am spoiled by my pastor. He understands women and ministers to them very well. Some of that may come from having two daughters and being the only male in the house!"

While many women praise their pastors, a large number desperately need counseling, but don't dare ask for help.

"There is no one to whom I can go for counsel, guidance, and true prayer," confesses an Arkansas woman, "because teaching the Word in our church seems so shallow and without impact."

Sadly, other surveys reflect this same sentiment.

PASTORAL COUNSELING HAS SOME DISADVANTAGES

Pastoral counseling serves as one way to help women who undergo pain and crisis. But it has some disadvantages. Consider the three disadvantages pastors most commonly voice:

1. *Time Constraints*

Pastors typically struggle with trying to juggle all of their responsibilities in the church. They often find that pastoral counseling can be a sinkhole that, if not carefully controlled, can consume all their time.

2. *Limited Understanding*

Pastors can't be "experts" in all areas of life. A pastoral counselor might have limited understanding about a particular problem in a woman's life and not fully know the best way to help her.

3. *A Church Member's Refusal to Pastoral Counseling*

Sometimes a woman will refuse her pastor's kind offer for counseling for several reasons. Some women don't want their pastors to know about their secret problems. An Oklahoma woman writes: "Christian women today aren't willing to share their past or present experiences for fear their pastor will think badly of them. Pastors might think we are less of a Christian because we have something in our past that is not pleasing."

Others fear their pastor might become their "knight in shining armor," and their need for his continued counsel will become a dependency. A woman from Minnesota writes: "I know of a lot of hurting women in the pews who want help. But because of fear, many women come to church and leave still 'hemorrhaging,' because of the 'wounds' in their lives."

Other women fear feeling sexually tempted when meeting alone with a pastor in a counseling session. Author Beverly White Hislop writes: "A woman experiencing emotional trauma or pain is a woman who is emotionally vulnerable. A woman in pain may wrongly interpret words and touch intended to offer solace. Her past grid may influence her to interpret expressions of tenderness by a male as a sexual advance."[2]

The wise pastor avoids a possibility of sexual misinterpretation when he incorporates some well-known ground rules into his pastoral counseling sessions. For instance, he invites a church staff member—who can keep confidences—into the office with him and the woman counselee. Or he asks the woman counselee to invite several of her friends into the session.

For these reasons and others, a pastor must never take personally a woman's refusal to accept his offer of personal counseling. When a woman in the church does initially agree to pastoral counseling, he shouldn't get discouraged if she postpones the appointment, or doesn't realize immediate relief from the help, or converts back to familiar, harmful behaviors.

In his book *No Perfect People Allowed*, John Burke writes: "Broken people are wounded people. Like abused puppies, they often run from those attempting to help them. Leaders must create a safe climate, so the healing work of God can begin in their lives. It will take patience and time. People will come and go, walking toward the light of freedom, then plunging back into the darkness. But they must see the church as a lighthouse; always there to lead them into the safe harbor of God's grace."[3]

Even if pastoral counseling is not the best option (for whatever reason), the church can still be a "lighthouse" and lead hurting women into the "safe harbor of God's grace."

HURTING WOMEN WANT *FEMALE* COUNSELORS

The vast majority of surveyed women ask specifically for *female* counselors. They feel they can communicate better with a woman than a man.

"My pastor recognizes the realities and limitations the church is so often faced with that are better addressed by women staff members, especially when counseling young girls and women," writes a Kentucky woman.

"Pastor," writes a Colorado woman, "please provide *female* lay counselors for women who are hurting or who need a listening ear."

Another writes: "We are too embarrassed to talk with a male about our personal problems, especially those intimate issues that relate only to women."

Women understand women because they experience the same life stages, deal with the same kinds of pain, and "speak the same language."

There's no way a male pastor can completely understand the mood swings of PMS, or the monthly painful menstrual cramps, or the "hot flashes" of menopause. Nor can he identify with a woman's heartache caused by infertility, divorce, miscarriage, or postpartum depression. One just cannot experience those things through textbooks. But another female can understand very well. She can sympathize *and empathize* with a hurting woman because she has most likely experienced the same or similar pain.

MEN AND WOMEN SPEAK DIFFERENT LANGUAGES!

Author Dr. John Gray is right on target when he states that "men are from Mars" and "women are from Venus." In his bestselling book, Gray makes the point that people from different planets will *obviously* speak different languages.

"Men mistakenly expect women to think, communicate, and react the way men do," writes Gray. "Women mistakenly expect men to feel, communicate, and respond the way women do. We have forgotten that men and women are supposed to be different."[4]

How do communication skills differ between men and women? "While Martians [men] tend to pull away and silently think about what's bothering them," Gray explains, "Venusians [women] feel an instinctive need to talk about what's bothering them."[5]

It's a simple concept, but profoundly true. When women face a dilemma, they need to talk about it. And talk and talk and talk. The more women talk about a problem, the more understanding they gain just from hearing themselves discuss it aloud. And when they talk, they want a listener — someone who will look them in the eye, and nod or grunt occasionally to prove they are listening. Through talking, women usually figure out the solution to the problem on their own. But first, they need to verbally express and carefully consider its every facet and every possible option to solve it.

When women talk through a problem, "solutions begin to emerge and simpler approaches appear as possibilities. It is as if stress catapults her into an emotional fog bank. Before she can navigate the course, she needs to clear the fog by talking her way through it. Her conversational roadmap can include God, friends, extended family, and her husband.... The key is she must talk her way out."[6]

While stressed and hurting women want a listener, they do not want a "fixer." Men want problems "summed up in a very small nutshell." Women don't. Men want an *acorn* of explanation — women want a *fully grown tree* of discussion! When pastors understand a female's need to talk, they wisely employ the practical biblical advice of James: "Everyone should be quick to listen [and] slow to speak" (James 1:19).

Women are different from men, and they communicate differently. Scripture explains it right from the beginning: "God created man in his own image, in the image of God he created him; *male and female he created them*" (Genesis 1:27, my emphasis).

For some reason, however, today's society is just discovering that men and women are different! Just look at the popular "male-female-communicating-together" books that line the bookstore shelves: *Men Are from Mars, Women Are from Venus*; *Men Are Like Waffles, Women Are Like Spaghetti*; *Men Are Clams, Women Are Crowbars*, and others. Each book attempts to solve the communication differences/problems between "Martians, waffles, and clams" and "Venusians, spaghetti, and crowbars"!

Sometimes a woman experiences a problem that requires numerous counseling sessions, and a great deal of extended time. Because of other responsibilities, pastors cannot give that much time to an individual member. He might also feel inadequately qualified to handle some serious crisis situation. In these cases, a pastor has two good options: he can recommend professional counseling outside the walls of the church, and/or arrange lay counseling within the congregation.

PROFESSIONAL COUNSELING

The prepared pastor keeps a well-researched and frequently updated list of professional *Christian* counselors — both male and female.

"People typically enter [professional] counseling because they are hurting, frustrated, or feeling overwhelmed by a problem," writes Rob Jackson. "In my experience, most of these circumstances are based in wounded relationships between husbands and wives and parents and children. And … one or more persons in these relationships may be experiencing *intrapersonal* difficulties, including mood disorders like depression and anxiety, addictions, or situational stressors like work or school."[7]

The pastor can discern a woman's need for professional help and then, if necessary, place her with a Christian counselor. I emphasize *Christian* counselor because the difference between secular counseling and Christian counseling is like the difference between waffles and spaghetti, clams and crowbars, Martians and Venusians.

"Secular counseling is grounded in humanism, and most often seeks to help a person adjust to difficult circumstances…. The end goal will most likely be some type of adaptation that provides symptom relief." Christian

---

counseling, on the other hand, "is grounded in the Bible, and most often seeks to help a person embrace the pain of his experience through a personal relationship with Jesus Christ.... The end goal ... will be a greater knowledge and enjoyment of God not based on circumstances."[8]

Carolyn Custis James states the difference eloquently when she writes about the deep theological roots of genuine Christian joy—the ultimate goal of every Christian counseling experience:

> Christian joy is more than a mood swing or a shift in hormone levels. Nor is it, as some have suggested, a choice or a duty to be happy, at least on the outside, even when we're miserable inside. True joy springs irrepressibly from the heart and is always rooted in our theology. Which explains why joy can appear in the middle of a crisis and coexist with pain, brokenness, grief, or loneliness. *Joy isn't grounded in our circumstances; it is grounded in the unchanging character of God....* But the most substantial reason for our joy is in the delight we find in God himself. Fixing our eyes on Jesus is, in itself, the single greatest cause for joy.[9]

WHY WOMEN MIGHT REFUSE PROFESSIONAL COUNSELING

Sometimes a pastor will recommend a professional counselor to a particular hurting woman in his church, but his advice and help will be refused. The reason for her refusal could be any one or a combination of the following:

- She can't afford the cost.
- She doesn't have the time.
- A friend had a bad experience with a professional counselor.
- She denies she has a problem.
- She considers her issues to be a normal part of a woman's life. Perhaps her mother or grandmother suffered with depression, grief, or guilt, and didn't think it was abnormal.
- She thinks she doesn't need the help of a counselor. She figures if she just works harder on the problem and focuses more on the solution, she can cure herself.
- She attaches a social stigma to one's need for counseling. Perhaps years ago her Aunt Jessie talked with a professional counselor, and family members whispered for years about Aunt Jessie's "mental illness."
- She thinks that, as a Christian with Jesus in her heart, seeking professional counseling shows a lack of faith.

- She wants to forget her problems and put them far behind her, instead of rehashing and reliving them again and again.

If, for whatever reason, the hurting woman in your congregation rejects the services of a professional counselor (and not every hurting woman will require a professional counselor), you have another good option—one that may prove more comfortable and just as effective.

FEMALE LAY COUNSELING

Lay counseling happens within the walls of your church. Some churches have members with educational backgrounds in counseling who are willing to offer their services to congregants. Other churches develop a lay counseling program. As a ministry of the church, they train spiritually mature members of the congregation to counsel the hurting church community.

Henri Nouwen describes "community" as a "fellowship of people who do not hide their joys and sorrows but make them visible to each other in a gesture of hope ... little 'stones' brought together in 'one big mosaic' portraying the face of Christ ... a fellowship of little people who together make God visible in the world."[10]

Lay counselors can multiply your church's ministry to hurting women. When your church community comes together to "portray the face of Christ," they can offer encouragement and support to women in pain. That's when healing starts to happen. The "little stones" come together in "one big mosaic" that ministers with strength and love and hope.

Professional counselors and lay counselors alike can be immense helps to pastors during times of congregational crisis. Also valuable are counselors from various organizations in the community. For instance, when church member Cindy calls you in tears to tell you her daughter just confessed to an unplanned pregnancy, you can enlist help from the local crisis pregnancy center. Or when Kayla cries into the phone at 2:00 a.m. and tells you her daughter just killed herself, you can enlist immediate aid from a local suicide trauma organization. Most organizations employ trained and specialized counselors who can expertly handle 9-1-1 type emergencies.

ELIZABETH'S STORY – A COUNSELING EMERGENCY

Carolyn, a stay-at-home mom, loved the Lord, her husband, and her five children. The family supported the church with their time, energy, money, and attendance. Fifteen-year-old daughter Elizabeth was active in the church's youth program.

Elizabeth left the Wednesday night church prayer meeting early, and walked home with a friend. Before they parted ways, Elizabeth told her friend she was going to finish cleaning her room and then kill herself. Her friend didn't take the threat seriously.

At 8:15 that evening, Carolyn came home from church, and found Elizabeth in her room, dead from a self-inflicted gunshot wound.

The youth at church later told Carolyn that Elizabeth often talked about suicide, but in a subtle, almost joking way. As early as six years before, Elizabeth had told a friend about finding a gun hidden in her parents' closet.

"We didn't tell any of our five children that we owned a gun," Carolyn told me. "We kept it trigger-locked, unloaded, and hidden in the closet, with the trigger-lock key in another part of the closet."

Elizabeth went to a lot of trouble to find the gun, bullets, and trigger-lock key.

A pretty girl, Elizabeth was dedicated to the Lord, active in church, successful in school, and musically talented. But she had severe physical problems caused by congenital birth defects. She had undergone major surgery several years before, and suffered chronic back pain.

"It is apparent to us now that Elizabeth had planned her death for some time," Carolyn said. "She made elaborate preparations in her room that Wednesday night. She placed her music awards neatly in a plastic laundry basket, turned photos of herself facedown, laid out clothes for her burial, and left a note."

The note said: "I love you all, and I'm so sorry. Elizabeth."

Needless to say, Elizabeth's suicide devastated her family, church family, and community. It left scores of hurting people in shock and disbelief. When word about Elizabeth's suicide spread, Carolyn's pastor immediately took charge. And he did everything right!

What the Pastor Did Right

First, the pastor ministered to her immediate family. Then he called the congregation and community together. They came to the church in droves — mothers, fathers, teachers, community leaders, classmates, church members, and friends. The pastor invited counselors from the local high school to counsel with Elizabeth's teenaged schoolmates and churchmates. He asked representatives from the city's suicide crisis center to come and talk openly about suicide. The counselors stayed long into the evening, meeting with individuals who needed to talk. One counselor described the people's mood at the meeting as "tense, somber, and serious. Some of the kids were hysterical and blamed themselves for Elizabeth's death," he said.

What Elizabeth's Parents Did Right

A few weeks later, the pastor asked Elizabeth's parents to speak to the church youth. He wanted them to explain how a child's suicide devastates a family, and how suicide is never the answer to a teenager's problems. Carolyn and her husband eagerly faced the church youth, and as honestly as they could, described their tragedy. They also told them *why* they thought Elizabeth had killed herself. They explained their daughter's birth defect and the physical and emotional pain it had caused her. They assured each young person there that they were in no way responsible for Elizabeth's death.

The pastor's thoughtful and immediate actions brought his congregation close together as they mourned Elizabeth and met to talk and pray. It showed the entire community "the face of Christ," and led to hope and healing.

The Pastor's Other Areas of Church and Community Healing

But the pastor didn't stop there. He also organized a series of age-appropriate workshops and seminars on the topic of suicide, and asked lay and professional counselors to speak. He invited church members, parents and grandparents of teens, and others who needed to learn about suicide prevention. The counselors taught them to recognize the warning signs of potential suicide, thus striving to eliminate the threat of possible "copy-cats." By bringing the tragedy into the open, the pastor removed much of the social stigma attached to suicide, and allowed members of church and community to feel more comfortable talking with each other about it. The tragedy also gave the pastor a unique opportunity to counsel, minister, teach, and train new lay counselors within the church.

Social Stigma Overcome

The social stigma of suicide can destroy grieving parents who already feel devastated by their child's untimely and unexpected death. One grieving mother told me: "I look into the eyes of my friends, family, neighbors, and fellow church members and wonder what they're thinking about me, about our family, about our parenting. People I have known for years have begun to avoid me, are careful not to make eye contact, and don't know what to say or do."

With the help of her pastor, Carolyn and her family found healing. Several months after Elizabeth's death, Carolyn wrote:

> In those dark days immediately following Elizabeth's death, I felt as if my very soul had been ripped apart. I felt like an empty shell of my former self; one merely going through the motions of living. At times I could not feel God's presence, the God who had always been there for me. He seemed so silent and distant, and I was too devastated even to pray for myself.
>
> Yet, somehow, in the middle of all this hopelessness and total despair, I began to feel little moments of comfort. The incredible hurt and pain were still there, but I began to feel God's presence again, maybe only for a few fleeting minutes, but I knew he was there, holding me up and walking beside me. Often I would receive a phone call or a note in the mail from a friend who had been praying for our family. Then I would think back on how the burden of pain and grief had seemed miraculously lifted for a time.[11]

THE COUNSELING ADVANTAGES OF A WOMEN'S MINISTRY

Another significant opportunity to offer support, prayer, and lay counseling comes through a church's women's ministry. I cannot express how important this program is to the pastor for ministering/counseling purposes. And it is of ultimate importance to the church's women. (Women's ministry can also assist the pastor in a number of other helpful ways: hospital visitation, food pantries, international student ministries, welcome and hospitality classes for new members, practical help for new mothers, international and local missions, used clothes closets, homeless outreaches, nursing home ministries, etc.)

An Alabama woman writes: "It would be a wonderful ministry for pastors to provide classes for hurting women in their churches in order to help women deal with various issues."

Classes in the form of seminars, workshops, Bible studies, and other settings can come under the umbrella of women's ministry. These teaching sessions can be led by professional counselors from the community and various organizations, as well as by church lay counselors and invited speakers/authors, Bible teachers, theologians, and others who are knowledgeable about the chosen subjects. Let's look briefly at each event format:

Seminars

A seminar typically is a one-time meeting for the women of the church to come together to hear a speaker/counselor discuss a particular topic or area of concern. It can last an hour or several hours. Seminar leaders sometimes break a large group into small groups to discuss the topic together in more detail.

The seminar also serves as an evangelical tool. Seminars opened up to the community will usually bring in unchurched women as well as members of your congregation. It's a wonderful way to reach those who might not, on their own, attend Sunday morning worship services. When unchurched women step into the seminar and are welcomed warmly by caring members, they most often return to church—and often they bring their families with them!

Workshops

A church might host multiple workshops led by invited speakers, authors, and professional or lay counselors. Workshops on different topics can occur simultaneously, allowing each woman to choose the one that most appeals to her and her present need. For instance, a day-long workshop on the topic of marriage might include individual sessions on communication, sexual problems, and true marital love. Workshops can valuably address a variety of issues, for example, dealing with depression, controlling anger, parenting teenagers, or reaching out to hurting women. Workshops, like seminars, can be opened up to unchurched women in the community.

Bible Studies

These ongoing classes might meet weekly—morning and/or evening—in the church facilities or in homes or other suitable offsite locations. Bible studies can be topical—covering subjects such as fear, finances, loneliness, prayer, and parenting—with the goal of helping women better understand what Scripture teaches about various everyday issues. Or they can be expository studies that encourage and teach women to study the Bible—book by book and/or verse by verse. Bible studies can run for six weeks, eight weeks, or indefinitely. They don't take the place of a well-organized Sunday school or adult education program, but they can greatly complement it, providing deeper insight into Scripture, a more relaxed atmosphere, and a greater length of time to study and discuss God's Word.

When women come together to study the Bible in organized seminars, workshops, and Bible studies, they form close bonds of friendship. They nurture and counsel each other. They walk together as friends through times of crisis, pain, and discouragement.

CHURCH WOMEN WANT WOMEN'S MINISTRY

Christian church women are begging for women's ministry programs that provide them opportunities to receive and give love, support, counseling, and practical help. These church programs, however, must be well organized and remain active. They also require spiritually mature *female* leaders and adequate church funding. They must reach out to women of all ages and all stages of life and circumstance.

"Our church has a very active women's ministry," writes one woman, "but not much is planned for older women."

Another writes: "There is a bit of frustration in my church about women's ministry. About two years ago, a program was started, but then we had a pastoral change. The women's ministry *female* leader left, and a *man* took her place. The program that had started for women, and seemed to be going so well, was sidelined during this transition."

An Illinois woman writes: "It has been my experience that church boards generally expect women's ministry functions to be self-supporting rather than viewing them as [worthy recipients of church budget funds]."

A woman from Oregon writes: "Ministry for women in the church is as important as children's ministry, youth ministry, men's ministry, and music ministry. I believe the heart of the home begins with the woman. If you have a woman being encouraged to grow in her love for God, you will have a happier home. It is the same for the church. If you have a vital women's ministry, you will have a happier, more productive church. I have heard time and time again how women's ministry women have reached out to those around them and brought them to a saving knowledge of Jesus Christ."

From Virginia: "Most churches are providing nice women's ministries now, and these are generally done by women in the church rather than paid staff. Pastors should support, encourage, and understand the importance of women's ministries. Recognize them from the pulpit—the hours of volunteer work that go into putting on high-quality events. Realize that when women come, children come, then men generally come."

From Florida: "I believe that simply asking a church lady, who is willing to organize women's events in her spare time, just isn't enough. It will take guidance and leadership from a staff member to organize a consistent women's ministry."

Another exclaims: "Women are not experiencing biblical community. Due to the busyness of life and geographic challenges, we do not experience 'doing life together' as the early church did. Women's ministry would bring us together!"

And finally, this encouraging response from a woman in Washington state: "Our pastor does a great job of supporting a thriving women's ministry program at our church. We focus on intensive Bible studies, as well as fellowship and involvement with church life as a whole. I am thankful he sees the importance of this ministry. Perhaps it would be good if all pastors knew the crucial role a well-founded and well-supported women's ministry program plays."

In the next chapter, we'll look at how the church can use the umbrella of women's ministry to assist hurting women through woman-to-woman mentoring, "shepherding programs," and friendship-building events.

Today's Christian woman wants her pastor to know that:

- She needs biblical counseling to help her and her family cope with unexpected crises and everyday problems.
- She often suffers in silence because she doesn't know how to seek biblical counseling through the church.
- If she doesn't get help, she worries about how unresolved pain might harm her physical, emotional, mental, and spiritual health.
- She appreciates you as her pastor and pastoral counselor, but often feels hurt and vulnerable. She might refuse to meet with you because she wants to avoid the risk of misinterpreted feelings and/or awkward situations.
- She doesn't want to offend you, but she feels more comfortable discussing personal and intimate issues with a female rather than a male.
- When she *does* talk with you, she doesn't necessarily want you to "fix" the problem, or give her solutions. She just wants you to listen.
- When she faces a problem, she needs to talk about it, to verbalize it for a period of time, so she can sort it out and solve it. She wants a caring and patient listener.
- When you recommend a professional counselor, she often has personal reasons why she doesn't accept, or follow up on, your offer.
- She likes the idea of lay counseling from within the congregation, and would greatly appreciate a female lay counselor.
- She asks you to support (financially and prayerfully) the church's women's ministry.
- If at all possible, she asks for a full-time, adequately paid female women's ministry coordinator.
- She wants you to help her reach out to hurting women throughout the church/community through topical seminars, workshops, and Bible studies; to provide a welcoming place to meet; and to supply adequate funding.
- She urges you to recognize the importance of the church's women's ministry—from the pulpit and in committee meetings—and to realize how an active women's ministry can benefit church women and the entire church body.

CHAPTER 4

"PASTOR, I YEARN FOR CHRISTIAN FRIENDS AND FELLOWSHIP"

> *We live in a highly fragmented, relationally isolated society. People move, change jobs, get divorced, commute hours each day, travel around the country weekly, then spend all their free time surfing through 1,700 cable channels and millions of Internet sites, and all at the cost of relationships. We have increased our financial capital, but it has cost us relational capital. Add to it the other societal trends of the past half-century, and you have a generation feeling painfully alone.*[1]

John Burke

WHEN A PASTOR and his congregation minister to a hurting woman, the whole church benefits. In the previous chapter, we looked at the value of pastoral, professional, and lay counseling, as well as the teaching and encouragement tools of church seminars, workshops, and Bible studies. In this chapter, we'll examine other avenues of help and healing for Christian women.

A WOMAN NEEDS FEMALE FRIENDS

Women today long for community, yet we live in "a culture of aloneness"—a "highly fragmented, relationally isolated society.... of people longing for community, but afraid to get close—surrounded by friends, feeling ever more alone."[2]

Isolation in our society has hurt women today. Even the busiest women are lonely. They need friends who can help them cope with today's fast-paced, mobile society. Women crave community—that special network of friends who genuinely care about, trust, and help each other. I heard this sentiment echoed in hundreds of survey responses.

"I believe isolationism is the number one problem women face today," writes a Florida woman. "In the hectic pace of today's world, the working woman has no time for interaction with other women; the stay-at-home mom feels isolated from other women. Job relocations have taken women far away from the support of the larger family."

Unlike men, many women do not function well without friends. Society seems to isolate women, not bring them together. But the church can bring women together, and in loving, caring, helping communities. Where society fails, the church flourishes. Churches have unique opportunities to be loving families to women today, as well as to their husbands and children. The church can become a woman's haven of healing, encouragement, and spiritual growth. It can become "community" to women stranded and lost in society's crowd of self-seeking, success-driven humanity.

A good Christian female friend can greatly change a woman's life. Just think of how a friend could reach out to Mary—the shy, lonely, newly widowed woman in your church. Friends could offer her good company and laughter. They could help wipe away Mary's tears and loneliness, and walk close beside her during that difficult first year after her husband's death.

Just think how a Christian friend could minister to Kayla, whose daughter, Marie, committed suicide. She could help Kayla feel less alone as she struggles with grief, confusion, and anger. She could offer Kayla a helping hand as Kayla assumes full responsibility for her daughter's children. Kayla needs a female friend who will listen to her frustration and pain, and who will be there when she needs to talk.

WHY WOMEN NEED FRIENDS

God created women with relational natures. Loving friendships bring most women great fulfillment, satisfaction, and joy. Women share more than conversation and ideas and thoughts with their friends. They often share their very hearts.

New studies from the University of Iowa show that when women feel a strong sense of friendship with others, they enjoy better health. The research revealed that patients with ovarian cancer who had satisfying relationships and a strong sense of connection to others possessed more vigorous "natural killer" cell activity at the site of the tumor than those who didn't have close, healthy social ties. (These desirable white blood cells kill cancerous cells as part of the body's immune system.)[3]

"Women are keepers of each other's secrets, boosters of one another's wavering confidence, co-conspirators in life's adventures. Through laughter, tears and an inexhaustible river of talk, they keep each other well, and make each other better."[4]

Most women thrive in healthy Christian friendships with other women.

THE NEED FOR TRUST

At the heart of every woman-to-woman friendship is the essential element of trust. Intimate relationships come only in the atmosphere of genuine concern for each other's well-being, and deep-rooted trust. When I confide in a friend, I must know, without a doubt, she will keep my confidence. If she shares my confidence with another person, I feel betrayed, and that friendship-trust is severed. While I *will* forgive her, I probably won't ever confide in her again. I might not even maintain the friendship.

Some women have been so betrayed and hurt in life, they don't trust anyone anymore. They deny themselves close friendships, and choose instead to relate to others in superficial, surface ways. They talk about the weather, not their feelings. They discuss politics, not their innermost hopes and dreams. They speak about religion, not their intimate personal faith in Jesus Christ. They keep their heart closed, and refuse entrance to all. Because their hurt and lack of trust run so deep, some women convince themselves they don't need friends. Yet inside, their heart screams for community and belonging.

A wise pastor will put emphasis and energy into creating special times of fellowship for his female congregants. He will also strive to develop a feeling of "family" within his congregation.

A woman from Maine writes: "A church needs to be an extended family for church women. Close relationships help a woman stay grounded."

A healthy congregational family will love and care for every member. Each will own a special place of importance and value. When decisions are made, the needs of each member will be thoughtfully and prayerfully considered. A healthy family works together for the enrichment of everyone, and ministers personally to all those who hurt. Members give and receive, and make each other feel safe, accepted, respected, and needed. A loving church family provides a haven for its members, and Christ is the head of that haven.

Perhaps that's what Jesus means when he prays that "all [believers] may be one, Father, just as you are in me and I am in you ... that they may be one as we are one: I in them and you in me" (John 17:21–23).

Through the familial "oneness" of the church, women can reach out to women and, in Christ, they can find health and healing.

FOUR EFFECTIVE WAYS TO BUILD "ONENESS"

Some churches have discontinued Bible-teaching Sunday school programs. For those churches that have continued the program, Sunday school has one great disadvantage, at least as far as building strong female friendships goes, and that's lack of time for fellowship. Female bonding and friendship-trust take time and talk. Sunday school should be a time for serious Bible study and prayer, and lengthy "meetings and greetings" take away from its main focus. But Sunday school can be complemented by during-the-week times of fellowship through mentoring and shepherding programs and well-organized events. Let's look at each of these ideas individually.

Woman-to-Woman Mentoring

In Titus 2:3–4, the apostle Paul urges Pastor Titus (whom he leaves on Crete to nurse infant churches) to "teach the older women ... to teach what is good. Then they can train the younger women."

Paul's advice is based on this principle: When spiritually mature, older, and more life-experienced women provide necessary instruction to younger women, these young women grow spiritually deeper in Christ, and learn basic life-ministering skills.

Almost gone are the days when young women stay in their home community, surrounded by wise mothers and grandmothers and aunts. These days, when girls reach age eighteen, they head off to college and leave their extended families behind. After college, they may marry and/or choose careers that forever keep them geographically distant from their female elders.

That's what happened to me. I married at nineteen, left my mother and grandmother and aunts in Chattanooga, Tennessee, and, with my new husband, I moved to Boston, Massachusetts, some 1,200 miles away. Although busy with work and school, I felt painfully alone, lost, and homesick. I missed valuable learning experiences my mother and grandmother would have provided. Except to visit, I never got back "home" again.

While far from home, however, God put three older, wiser, and more spiritually mature women in my life: Doris Moore Hughston, Mary Ann

Allen, and Peg Milley. Each woman became a close friend and trusted mentor. I learned firsthand about the beauty and benefits of the "Titus 2 woman."

To mentor someone means to disciple her one-on-one.

"A godly older woman will point the younger woman to the only One who will never disappoint her and who is completely trustworthy in any and all of life's situations," writes Vickie Kraft in *Women Mentoring Women*. "She will instruct her from the Bible and from her own life experience in coming to know Him better."[5]

Jesus mentored a group of men and women during his three-year ministry travels. He taught and counseled them, prayed with and for them, and protected and equipped them to continue his work after his death. At least eleven of his male disciples (Judas excluded) and probably all of his female disciples benefited greatly from his mentoring.

According to Luke, "The Twelve were with him, and also some women who had been cured of evil spirits and diseases: Mary (called Magdalene) from whom seven demons had come out; Joanna the wife of Cuza, the manager of Herod's household; Susanna; and many others. These women were helping to support them out of their own means" (Luke 8:1–3).

The women Jesus taught and mentored proved to be strong witnesses for him during his ministry and after his resurrection.

"Rabbis conventionally taught only males," writes Dr. Fisher Humphreys, "and Jesus was different in this regard ... because he taught women."

"On one occasion," explains Dr. Humphreys, "when Jesus was visiting in the home of two sisters who were his friends, one of them, Martha, criticized her sister Mary for listening to Jesus rather than working in the kitchen. Behind Martha's criticism of Mary lay the conventional understanding that the teaching of rabbis was not for women. Jesus reprimanded her and told her that, in learning from Jesus, Mary has chosen the better part, which will not be taken away from her" (Luke 10:42).[6]

Though Jesus himself gives us the example of mentoring, many churches still depend solely on Sunday school to provide fellowship and discipling/mentoring to its women.

In researching his book, *High Expectations: The Remarkable Secret for Keeping People in Your Church*, Dr. Thom Rainer found few churches that "offered some type of one-to-one mentoring or discipleship ministry."

In his follow-up interviews with church leaders, many told him "their Sunday school classes provided the ongoing discipleship emphasis," and they "saw little need in creating yet another time-consuming program."

Dr. Rainer states: "Overall,... only one-fourth of the churches offered one-to-one mentoring or discipleship." And he adds, "Conventional wisdom states that unmet needs are often stated as the reason people leave the church or become inactive."[7]

Without programs designed to join them together in mentoring, fellowship, and discipleship, church women will not have their spiritual needs met. And, as already noted, the Sunday school hour alone cannot accommodate all these needs. Time won't allow it.

An Ohio woman writes: "The church has a lack of mature female Christian role models. We need mature sisters in the faith to help us younger women navigate life."

A woman from Oklahoma agrees: "We need spiritual guidance from mature and willing female mentors who have walked the same paths we now walk."

Another advises: "Our church women—both single and married—crave nurture through women's fellowship and mentoring groups."

When an older, more spiritually mature woman mentors a younger woman, both benefit. The spiritually mature woman is given the opportunity to use her God-given gifts in ministry. The younger woman becomes more spiritually mature, and learns the gifts that enable her to become a future mentor to another young woman.

To complement the woman-to-woman mentoring program, pastors might also introduce the idea of the "shepherding" woman.

The Shepherding Woman

Whereas woman-to-woman mentoring programs team up an older woman with a younger woman for the purpose of *teaching*, a shepherding program teams a woman with another woman for the purpose of *ministering*. The "shepherd" becomes the woman's "helper," walking beside her, aiding her in practical ways, and ministering to her emotional and spiritual needs.

Shepherds listen, and friendships happen. Both shepherding and mentoring work better when women "teams" develop naturally, rather than by assignment. Women's ministry events—banquets, luncheons, retreats, and other fellowship times—draw women together and encourage friendships naturally.

Often, shepherds can gently bring women into Sunday school who "just don't seem to 'fit' into Sunday school," and are therefore not involved. Shepherds can introduce them to other women in the class, and make them feel more welcomed and comfortable.

In a sense, shepherding and pastoral care are the same.

"Pastoral care to women includes elements of mentoring, pastoral counseling, spiritual direction, and discipleship," writes Beverly White Hislop. "These comprise the components of shepherding. So pastoral care and shepherding essentially are synonymous."

Hislop continues: "[The shepherd] may be called on to facilitate, coach, listen, pray, or transmit information.... This relationship may even develop to a level of mentor or disciple.... The greatest distinction of a shepherd is that she is a woman who intentionally provides the comfort and understanding that fosters healing and growth."[8]

"Women have needs that need to be addressed," a Tennessee woman writes. "There needs to be opportunities for women to be ministered to by other women, especially strong Christian women. If we were helped and encouraged in this way, we would be stronger for the church. We could contribute more, for we would feel more confident and prepared. Most women lack contact with a close-knit person (or persons) with which to share life on a regular basis."

Fortunate is the woman who is given the gift of a strong Christ-centered shepherd who closely befriends her and gently leads her toward Christ and healing.

The Wounded Healer

A mentor or shepherd can become a "wounded healer" to a hurting woman in your congregation if she has experienced and recovered from the same or similar pain.

When Naomi's fifty-two-year-old husband died suddenly from a massive heart attack, she was overwhelmed with grief. She experienced all the painful symptoms of mourning—tightness in her chest and throat, insomnia, weight loss, headaches, anger, resentment, bitterness, irritability, and mood swings. She lost all interest in things she previously loved, such as reading, shopping, and cooking. She often felt disoriented, unable to concentrate or focus. She withdrew completely from social activities.

Pastor Ted knew the symptoms and stages of grief. He met with Naomi and prayed with her. Then he introduced her to Marla, a spiritually strong Christian woman whose husband, years ago, also had died suddenly. Marla became Naomi's close friend and wounded healer. She walked Naomi through the grief process, and Naomi emerged with a renewed trust in God, a greater faith, and a best friend. Naomi told Pastor Ted that one day she herself wanted to be a wounded healer to another hurting widow.[9]

Wounded healers can shepherd a fellow struggler with great understanding and empathy. Pastors, church members, and women's ministries can bestow the gift of introduction and healing when they bring together a wounded healer and a hurting woman.

Many churches are filled with Christian women who have the time and crave the opportunity to help another woman find healing in Christ. Sometimes, however, church women may not be able to give the amount of time needed to a woman in a mentoring/shepherding situation because of other urgent schedule demands. Some pastors can't find "enough committed disciplers who are willing to give the hours necessary to such a labor-intensive responsibility." When they do find a wounded helper, she is often times a "discipler [who is one] of the busiest church members," discovered Dr. Thom Rainer as he researched his book, *Effective Evangelistic Churches*.[10]

When female mentors, shepherds, and wounded healers are not readily available, the pastor has another good option: support groups.

CHURCH- AND COMMUNITY-SPONSORED SUPPORT GROUPS

Support groups strive to bring together women who are undergoing similar painful experiences. Within the small groups, women can share information, testimonials, techniques for coping, and so on. They can talk, listen, and befriend each other. Meeting once a week or once a month, a support group brings healing to a hurting woman, encourages maintenance to a healing woman, and gives the healed woman opportunities to minister to others.

Churches can start and support these groups, using Scripture as a foundation for healing and encouraging a woman's closer walk with Christ. Community support groups might not offer a scriptural foundation, but they *can* bring women together and in contact with others who journey through similar circumstances.

Support groups most often join together women of all ages, stages, occupations, and races. They meet for a common purpose and to pursue a common goal. They encourage women to be open and honest, to admit they have a problem, and to be transparent within the group.

"Women need friendships with other women of all ages," an Ohio woman writes. "Anything the church can do to encourage multigenerational friendships is important."

"I want my pastor to know the importance of community among church women," writes a woman from Minnesota. "It is hard for women in many churches to find true community because women can have difficulty being transparent in group settings. Sometimes we are too worried about what others think, and it keeps us from truly being who we are."

In addition to support groups, another good idea for fostering female friendships (in a Christ-centered environment) is the church-sponsored women's event.

CHURCH-SPONSORED EVENTS FOR WOMEN

A woman from Michigan wants her pastor to know "how important it is to women to have their emotional and spiritual needs met through fellowship with other Christian women," and that "there is a lack of Christian fellowship among women."

Women enjoy getting together with other women to share fellowship. Under the women's ministry "umbrella," a church can provide and host suppers, luncheons, retreats, and other events that bring Christian women together. Events can be as fancy as an afternoon English-style tea or banquet, or as simple as a picnic or potluck supper. Some churches organize retreats for women at local campgrounds, or at nearby hotels with large meeting rooms. These retreat-events can last for several hours or for several days. They may include Bible study, a special invited speaker, quiet time, prayer, and fellowship.

Church-sponsored events fill the vacuum in the lives of many Christian women, especially those who have few Christian friends or are isolated and lonely.

"Women are highly relational," writes an Oregon woman. "They seek places to form connections with other women to talk about their everyday lives. Women *will* find a forum in which to fellowship, so churches should make sure they offer this opportunity in a Christian environment. Plant mature Christian women in these groups, invest God's Word in their lives, and the church, community, and nation will be transformed!"

Not only do women crave Christian fellowship with other women, they also yearn to study God's Word. In the next chapter, we'll look at ways the church can develop its women into spiritually mature giants!

Today's Christian woman wants her pastor to know that:

- Women are relational in nature; they need other female friends.
- A hurting woman needs a spiritually mature female friend who can minister to her, listen to her, advise her, and walk beside her during her pain.
- Younger women need older, more experienced, spiritually mature women to mentor, teach, help, and set a godly life-example for them—as Paul encourages in Titus 2.
- A female "shepherd" can greatly help and encourage a hurting woman.
- Women need church and community support groups, so they can both give and receive help and hope.
- Women need restful retreats from busy schedules and heavy workloads. They desire Christian fellowship with other women.
- "Wounded healers" can offer women encouragement and healing through Christ and their own loving presence.
- Women who have suffered painful situations are better able to minister to women who are suffering the same or similar situations.

"PASTOR, I CRAVE BIBLE STUDY AND SPIRITUAL GROWTH"

A woman's theology can make all the difference in how well she fights the battles that are part of God's plan for her. Sometimes theology is all we have in the war zone.[1]

Carolyn Custis James

I AM SHOCKED and greatly saddened when I see photos of hungry, starving people, whether the survivors of World War II German and Japanese concentration camps or twenty-first century poverty and famine victims in Haiti, Africa, and Bangladesh. It breaks my heart to know some nations battle obesity while other nations battle starvation. It also amazes me to see people starving by the roadside in India while "beef" freely roams the streets. Or fancy hotels in Mexico serving "death-by-chocolate" desserts while a baby starves in a next-door slum. Why do some need kitchen sink garbage disposals to eliminate leftover food, while others must search city trash bins for thrown-away crumbs? Surely we have the technology and necessary resources to feed a hungry world! But why don't we do it?

WOMEN TODAY ARE SPIRITUALLY STARVING

Human beings need food and physical nourishment to live and grow. Yet even more important than physical life, they need God's Word to live and grow spiritually. As much as the body needs meat, food is temporary. The soul needs to feed on Scripture—it is eternal.

All around me I see women who exist with the barest scriptural basics, and live with thin skin stretched over bones of spiritual malnourishment. Women battle spiritual starvation in a society filled with Bibles! On many corners of our community and city streets, we find large elaborate buildings—built for the worship of God and the study of Scripture. As a nation, we possess all the necessary resources to feed starving people the life-giving meat of Scripture, yet hungry people search the trash bins of secularism in search of spiritual food.

Women today are spiritually starving! In a society spilling over with biblical resources, women are not being fed enough to grow and sustain their spiritual lives.

In survey after survey, Christian women express a deep hunger for theological doctrine—Bible study. Living in a culture that puts little emphasis on absolute truth, women desperately want to know the ultimate truth of God's Word. I watch and wonder as women today are enticed and seduced by Eastern religion's superstitious nonsense, and are being caught in the web of witchcraft, magic, and Wicca. In Christ, and through God's Word, we have the answer to today's spiritual famine among women. Yet so often, we are not feeding them.

A woman from Tennessee writes: "I want my pastor to know that women today need a clear interpretation of Scripture. We women fight constantly against the subtle pressures of culture.... We need to have clear definitions so we can guide and influence our culture by Scripture."

A Virginia woman expresses similar sentiments: "Pastor, show us how to be godly in an ungodly world! With all the things that women have to handle these days—like being a wife, mother, financial supporter, church volunteer, etc., it is hard to remain godly. Our children come home with ungodly words and actions, and it is our job to mold them and make them into what God wants them to be."

Another writes from North Carolina: "How can I live out what God's Word says in a world that is telling me to do the opposite? How can I stay continually connected to Christ in a world of distractions?"

Christian women around the country confess they feel the strong pull of a secular world, and they need scriptural guidance to counteract and overcome that pull. But, they cry, "We just aren't getting that guidance."

THE DRY SAND OF SPIRITUAL DESERT

"The number one problem church women face today is they have bought into the lies of our culture. I believe that too often the church culture doesn't look much different from the secular culture," writes the single mother of two small children.

An Oklahoma woman admits that she sees today's Christian women "conforming themselves to secular standards of mind and heart rather than biblical truth."

"We receive double messages—from society and the church. The Bible is the only place we can get clear answers. But we experience a constant battle every day to stay in God's will, in a society that doesn't understand, or care to understand, our walk with God," writes a New Englander.

Another writes from Mississippi: "Finding our identity in Christ is the number one problem we women face. I believe we search for our identity in everything and everyone except God. So many women believe their identity is in their job, their husband's job, their children, their social status, etc. Discovering who we are as women in Christ can be one of the most joyful, freeing, confidence-building things a woman can do."

It's true. We live in a time of intense spiritual hunger. Women are looking for answers, and sometimes they look in all the wrong places.

"People are thirsting for the sacred, the mysterious, the mystical. They are looking for more than a good job, a full closet, and a balanced checkbook."[2]

In a nation flowing with the pure mountain streams of God's true spirituality, we are too often offering women the hot dry sand of spiritual desert.

CONSUMING SPIRITUAL "FLUFF"

A number of surveyed women express their frustrations with "spiritual fluff." They want scriptural "meat," not "whipped cream." They are tired of church-sponsored fashion shows, cook-offs, and home decorating classes. The secular world constantly offers them fashion, food, and furnishings, and does it much better than the church can!

One woman writes: "There is a willingness to settle for the trivial, which is often encouraged by the nature of many women's ministries and by the wider society."

Says a Georgia woman: "I see the tendency for women to focus on themselves rather than on the purpose for which the church was formed. I have watched women's ministry emphases shift to such things as fashion, decorating, entertaining, and health issues. Surely, these things are less important than their eternal purpose!"

One woman writes about a women's event her church's women's ministry planned on a Saturday: "We were so excited," she said. "We had a whole Saturday to study God's Word. All of us mothers hired babysitters for our kids, put aside our Saturday chores, gathered up our Bibles and notebooks, and arrived early to get upfront seats. The church had invited two Christian speakers, and we could hardly wait to 'sit at their feet.'"

Imagine the women's disappointment when the main speaker was a woman who for three hours shared her all-consuming hobby of flea-market shopping!

"We listened to the speaker tell about all the stuff she had found at flea markets around the country. We sat there with closed Bibles on our laps and a vacuum in our hearts, and we listened respectfully as she enlightened us on useless 'treasures.' We were hungry for Real Treasure—the Treasure that lasts forever—God's Word. But we didn't get it. We craved spiritual direction and God's encouragement to get us through another demanding week. Instead, we heard about cheap 'finds' at flea-market prices."

After lunch, many of the women had to meet babysitters or go to work, so they left before the second speaker came to the podium. With only half the group remaining, and about twenty minutes of time left, the second speaker asked the women to open their Bibles. She then began to read about Jesus, the Good Shepherd, from John 10. She explained the text, and told the women of God's love and Christ's sacrifice and salvation. Then she asked each woman to bow her head, close her eyes, and to silently talk with God. While the women prayed, the speaker walked quietly through the room, stopped and touched each woman's shoulder, and prayed briefly with her. One by one each woman received spiritual encouragement, and the aroma of God's Spirit filled the room like a loaf of fresh bread baking in the oven.

WOMEN WANT TO HEAR ABOUT JESUS!

Pastor, when Christian women make complicated arrangements at home and work in order to study God's Word at church, they do not want to hear about the latest and greatest recipes or shoe styles. They want to hear about Jesus! We often think we can somehow entice women into coming to church by putting on a fancy fashion show or teaching them how to arrange flowers. While we might bring hurting women through the church doors, they leave no more spiritually nurtured than when they came. When we do evangelism by throwing church Super Bowl bashes, we may bring spiritually hungry people into the building, but they leave spiritually empty. We often treat God's Word as if it isn't powerful enough itself to bring people into the church.

An Alabama woman writes: "I desire to be challenged in thinking critically about faith and in pursuing God wholly. While women's ministry events are good and can help build up the body, they are often 'watered down,' in my observation. They are not challenging women to selfless, sacrificial discipleship. I would like to see pastors taking the lead in guiding the women of their congregations to be keenly interested in how a relationship with Christ calls them to look beyond themselves to a world in need."

Today's Christian woman is tired. She is hurting. She wants and desperately needs God's truth and answers to life's eternal questions. She wants to know her unique purpose. She wants to reach out and minister to others. We do women no favors when we take their valuable time and serve them spiritual "sugar" instead of scriptural "protein"! A little sugar might taste good every now and then, but we don't want a constant diet of it. We need protein for growth and sustenance!

Women yearn to learn about God: Who is he? Why did he create me? Does he really love me? Is eternal life fact or fiction? Who is Jesus in relationship to God? What do words like *atonement* and *justification* and *sanctification* mean? What must I do to get to heaven?

Women yearn to ask questions about prayer: What is it? How do I do it? Does God hear my prayers? How do I pray when God seems silent? Do my prayers ever change God's mind? How do I pray when I am hurting?

Women yearn to know if they have an eternal purpose in life: Why am I here? What should I be doing? Did God give me spiritual gifts? How can I discern my gifts and develop them to use in his kingdom?

Women crave fellowship with spiritually mature women who can guide them, encourage them, and give them spiritual advice and direction. Our job is to tell women today they "were created to know God, to return God's love, and to enjoy communion with God."[3]

Again and again the women I surveyed admit they ache for deep theology.

"Teaching the Word in our church seems so shallow and without impact," one woman sadly writes.

From Minnesota: "Women desperately need a real relationship with God. We need to know that God is our best friend—that he comforts, gives wisdom, direction, guidance, strength, and joy to us for the hard journey of life."

From Texas: "Women need to know God. They need theology. They need to know that God is omniscient, omnipresent, omnipotent, and that he loves them and cares for them. They need to know that God will never leave them."

Hundreds of women responded to my survey in this way. They want to know the proof of God's Word, and how it relates to their lives as grown, responsible Christian singles, wives, and mothers loaded down with huge responsibilities to spiritually educate the next generation.

A woman from Oregon writes: "We don't all like elementary 'fill in the blank' Bible studies. We want to learn at a [deeper] theological level!"

A Tennessee woman writes: "We love theology! We hunger for the deep things of God's Word. Move on from the basic 'milk' and give us a hearty diet of spiritual 'meat.' In Scripture we receive the resources for 'hanging tough' during life's trials. From Scripture, preeminently, we learn about our King, how his kingdom should function, and how to be thoughtful, discerning kingdom citizens in the here and now. Help us become better students of the Bible!"

A Florida woman agrees: "Women today are hungry for the meaty Bible studies and significant church involvement that goes deeper than many of the women's ministry offerings. We need God's Word!"

When we give women "fluff theology," we mentally reduce them to children with simple minds and short attention spans. We can give the impression that women can't comprehend complicated theology, that their minds aren't developed enough to understand deep, eternal doctrine. We quote *Chicken Soup for the Soul* when women beg for C. S. Lewis's *Mere Christianity,* J. I. Packer's *Knowing God,* and St. Augustine's *Confessions.*

A Midwestern woman writes: "There is a lack of serious biblical under-standing among women even in churches in which I would expect the opposite. There is a famine for the hearing of the Word of the Lord even in Bible churches.... This tells me that the churches trivialize women's needs and gifts, and women themselves don't recognize the problem in many cases. Talking *about* the Bible, or tacking a few verses on a *Reader's Digest*–type talk, is not taking the Scriptures seriously."

A woman from Tennessee writes: "Often, even among the most brilliant, godly ministers, is the implicit (sometimes explicit) suggestion that women are not intelligent enough to know about the Bible and theology. In discussions or question sessions, they sometimes seem surprised that a woman can articulate a precise, cogent statement regarding spiritual things."

Let me note before I go on that some women have been so overexposed to spiritual fluff instead of God's Word, they go to church expecting it. They have been taught little theological doctrine, and much more enjoy the "cruise-ship entertainment" weekend worship service. When their jobs transfer them to different parts of the country, and they join Bible-teaching churches, they feel at a loss to understand the new, deep concepts. Pastors often wrestle with spiritually immature church members' demands for entertainment when they yearn to teach them spiritual truth and doctrine.

JESUS ELEVATED WOMEN AND RESPECTED THEIR MINDS

The religious Jews of Jesus' day considered women to be chattel—insignificant property, possessing less credibility and value than their livestock. And the "enlightened" Romans of that time held women in even less regard, fathers often exposing their infant daughters to death by wild beasts or throwing them into the Tiber River.

In comparison, Jesus' attitude was nothing less than revolutionary.

He once stopped his temple teaching to heal a crippled woman—an act that infuriated the religious leaders. They complained that healings should not take place on the Sabbath, yet they really thought the woman not worth the attention and concern of Rabbi Jesus. That's when Jesus looked them in the eye, confronted their prejudices, and proved to them the woman had great value.

Jesus asked them: "Doesn't each of you on the Sabbath untie his ox or donkey from the staff and lead it out to give it water?" In other words, "Do you not value your livestock, and treat them with compassion and kindness—even on the Sabbath?"

Then he dropped a bombshell—the ultimate insult: "Then should not this woman, *a daughter of Abraham*, whom Satan has kept bound for eighteen long years, be set free on the Sabbath day from what bound her?"

Luke tells us that when Jesus said those words, all his opponents were "humiliated."

Why? Because Jesus dared to call this "insignificant" sick woman a "daughter of Abraham"! *Daughter of Abraham!* It's the only place in the entire Bible that places a woman in the same familial position as the "sons of Abraham." In essence, Jesus placed prestigious religious leaders (men) and a sick, crippled woman in the same social status—and on the same intellectual and spiritual level—as legitimate brothers and sisters of their father, Abraham (see Luke 13:10–17).

Charles Colson writes of Jesus, "No other person in human history has done as much to make it possible for women to realize their full potential as image bearers of God. He spoke directly to women in public at a time when this was not acceptable, a time when much of the world considered women to be little more than personal possessions.... Jesus' relationship with women was one of tenderness, caring, and concern; he treated them with absolute equal dignity."[4]

"Christianity has always elevated women!" explains author Diane Passno. "'There is neither Jew nor Greek, slave nor free, male nor female, for you are all one in Christ Jesus' (Galatians 3:28). Christ had a unique relationship with women. He 'connected' with them emotionally and spiritually. He elevated them ... he took care of them ... he talked to them ... he understood them.... We have so much evidence in Scripture of a risen Savior who honors women, understands them emotionally and physically, and answers their prayers daily."[5]

In her book, *Lost Women of the Bible*, Carolyn Custis James writes: "Women weren't ancillary, but crucial to Jesus. He didn't give them small jobs. He gave Mary two of the most significant—as the first witness to his resurrection and as an apostle to the apostles.... One of the first matters of business when Jesus appeared to his male disciples was to establish the testimony of the women (Luke 24:22–27). He had already elevated women by including them as his disciples. Now he affirmed their ministries too. They were his messengers. He gave them his word, and their message carried his authority."[6]

Throughout the Gospels, Jesus constantly encourages and affirms the women he encounters. We've already seen how, in Luke 10:38–42, Jesus praised Mary—who sat at his feet and soaked up his theology, desperately trying to quench her thirst for God's Word.

"Mary has chosen what is better, and it will not be taken away from her," Jesus told a worried and upset Martha. In doing so, he reaffirmed the eternal nature of theology over the temporal nature of food.

"Three things caused Mary to sit at our Lord's feet," wrote the fourteenth-century German theologian Meister Eckhart. "The first was that God's goodness had embraced her soul. The second was a great, unspeakable longing: she yearned without knowing what it was she yearned after, and she desired without knowing what she desired! The third was the sweet consolation and bliss that she derived from the eternal words that came from Christ's mouth."[7]

"More than simply granting women permission to learn as his disciples, Jesus calls Mary, Martha, and the rest of us to make knowing God our highest priority," writes Carolyn Custis James. "This call is in keeping with Jesus' well-established practice of challenging women to think more deeply about God. His ministry to women dispels the notion that women and theology do not mix. He wanted women to know God as well as the men did and took extraordinary measures to ensure that women heard and understood theology."[8]

If the world is a spiritual battleground, the women in your church need sharp swords to fight the war, not slingshots of superficiality. We've got the sword—the sharp two-edged Word of God—but, for some reason, we often keep it sheathed.

"I believe we have lost our First Love," laments an Alabama woman. "Unwittingly, we have allowed the cares and pleasures of this world to replace our devotion to our Lord and Savior. As Jesus told Martha (who was distracted by so 'many things'), Mary had chosen what was good and what could not be taken away. Women today are choosing what does not last, and we are wearing ourselves out pursuing and maintaining those things, all the while ignoring Jesus' plea to take up our cross daily and follow him."

A WOMAN'S PERSONAL TIME WITH GOD

Pastors must encourage women to create time in their busy days for *personal* Bible study and prayer. Weekly sermons, congregational prayer, and an hour of Sunday school just isn't enough for adequate spiritual growth. Some churches have discontinued Bible-based adult classes altogether. Other pastors offer Sunday school and other types of Bible-based classes, but complain that few congregants attend them. Somehow pastors must teach women to study God's Word on their own time, and to be devoted to quiet time and prayer.

A middle-aged single woman writes: "If we're honest with ourselves, our number one problem is a lack of *personal* holiness, which I believe is directly tied to a famine of prayer. We've filled up our lives with so much that God is being pushed to the margins."

An Ohio woman explains: "I think Christian women don't know the Word, and don't understand who their God really is."

Most survey respondents confess they "lack a regularly scheduled time of personal Bible study, prayer, worship, and meditation." Some warn about the dangers of depending on others to interpret Scripture for them instead of studying God's Word themselves.

"Church women need to be encouraged to *grow personally deep* in the Lord," writes a Michigan woman. "That may seem simplistic, but I feel that too many women lean completely on the church family to grow them spiritually. They need to hear from their pastor about the importance of *personally* digging deep for themselves. Women need to know and meditate on God's Word daily."

When women fail to make time for personal Bible study, they can be easily led away from the church and the Christian faith. And when they leave, they usually take a husband and children with them. A pastor can stress the importance of personal Bible study and prayer to the women of his church, and can teach them the urgency and necessity of scheduling *daily* appointments with God. These quiet study times don't just happen. Women must often move heaven and earth in order to *make them happen*! But the end result is well worth the effort!

A New York woman writes: "Women are not taking time to grow in their own relationship with God. With so many women doing so much outside the home (work, ministry, car pool, children's activities) it is difficult to slow down and say 'these next thirty minutes are for me to be with God.' We concentrate on serving our families, fellow church members, and communities. It is imperative that we take time to be aligned with our Lord first and continually."

"My biggest problem," writes a Georgia woman, "is taking time to study and meditate on God's Word so I can follow what God wants me to do, and not do just what others expect me to do." Another admits: "I continually face the problem of not being familiar enough with God's Word."

Again and again I heard the same sentiments expressed on surveys:

From Texas: "Women need more substance in God's Word. They need pastors and Sunday school teachers who know Scripture, who study and prepare lessons/sermons. Women have a lack of education of what the Scripture says. Women need to know where to go in God's Word to find answers."

From California: "I want to encourage my pastor to teach the hard truths. We need to be confronted, in love, with the truth of Scripture, even when it may step on some toes."

From Illinois: "Finding time for personal Bible study is challenging when everything around you demands so much time. Even on Sundays

during worship services, we are still mom, wife, sister, daughter, or whatever, and we don't always get our spiritual 'power surge' for the next week.
There are many times when I make a note of something the pastor said,
and I want to read more about it when I get home, and as soon as I prepare
to do so, I fall asleep in my Bible.... When I do have quiet time with God
though, I experience a wonderful sense of peace and relief."

A Nebraska woman agrees: "Despite the residual pain and heartache I
feel, careful discipleship by my pastor and church, and personal Bible study
have helped to bring about a total healing for me."

An Alabama woman writes: "The one thing that has encouraged me and
equipped me most to serve my family and others (the church, community,
etc.) is the Word—verse by verse study of the Holy Scriptures. Women
need to be encouraged to discipline themselves *personally* in this area, and
offered opportunities to fill their cups. As the old saying goes, 'If your cup
is empty, there's nothing to give.' Priority should be given to this."

A SENSE OF PEACE AND RELIEF

A "sense of peace and relief" comes to the woman who stays focused on
Christ, her Good Shepherd who knows her intimately and calls her by
name (John 10:3–5). Both personal and corporate Scripture study keeps
her running the race of faith instead of stumbling and falling on the side-
lines.

When a woman's time with Christ is limited, and she doesn't have a
regular diet of God's Word at church or home, she suffers. She suffers not
just spiritually, but in every part of her life. When she is not in the daily
"dead center" of God's Word, her entire life is "off center." Frustration
happens, relationships fracture, and she can quickly lose sight of the eternal because she is overwhelmed with the temporal things of life. She not
only forfeits her sense of peace and joy, but she forgets her purpose. Her
train either derails completely or switches to a track headed in the wrong
direction.

Author Brennan Manning acknowledges that Christians can fail to have
personal, or even corporate quiet prayer and adoration time, "silent rever-
ence," and "affectionate awe at the infinite goodness of God." He writes:

> Adoration which flows naturally from the aptitude to appreci-
> ate the grandeur of divine reality, is conspicuously absent in our
> prayer life. Quiet time is often not quiet. Our designated prayer
> time is generally consumed by hurried meditation on a Scripture

passage, a run through the Rolodex of persons to intercede/petition for, and occasional expressions of gratitude for the gifts of our lives — faith, health, family, and friends. The inner urgency to fall prostrate before the Infinite rarely intrudes on our consciousness. Recent studies have shown that the average congregation on a Sunday morning can tolerate only fifteen seconds of silence before someone feels compelled to break it with an announcement, a song, a prophecy, or whatever.[9]

Society, even church society, seems somewhat afraid of silence. Yet, in his own life, Jesus spent much time in solitude and silence. During one personal retreat, he went alone into the wilderness, and for forty days and forty nights, he practiced silence and personal prayer. During that time, Jesus went head-to-head with Satan, who tempted him with the *pleasures of the temporary*, while Jesus sought the *truths of the eternal*. Jesus knew his Scripture, and whenever Satan engaged him in battle, Jesus swung out his two-edged sword — God's Word — and won the war (Matthew 4:1 – 11).

Christian women today are surrounded on every side by Satan's temptations and subtle attempts to pull them away from God and his Word. Pastors must help protect the personal and corporate prayer/worship/Bible study time of these women. And there are some wonderful ways he can do that. A pastor can make sure every woman in his church has her own Bible (in a "user-friendly" translation), and he can teach her how to study it. He can encourage women to *make* time for personal Bible study, and teach them the value of solitude and silence in everyday life. He can ask the church to provide times of quiet retreat for women and organize discipleship classes and Sunday school programs that "fit" the women in the church.

SUNDAY SCHOOL, A PROVEN SOURCE OF SPIRITUAL INSTRUCTION

Since the late 1700s, the church has depended on Sunday school to educate children and adults theologically. While in previous chapters we noted some of the limitations of Sunday school in ministering to women in need of counseling and female fellowship, the advantages of this centuries-old institution (or whatever modern derivative we want to call it) should not be overlooked as part of full-faceted church experience each weekend.

When members get to class on time, meet and greet *briefly*, and then begin serious Bible study, the hour can be quite productive. A theologically knowledgeable and spiritually mature teacher can cover a significant portion of Scripture, have adequate discussion time, and lead the class in serious prayer.

An Oklahoma woman agrees: "We need to be fed the Word of God—spiritual food for the pressures and temptations of life, whether we are single, widowed, or married."

"I have wonderful pastors who are men of God," writes an Oregon woman. "I know they have hearts for discipleship, and want spiritual growth for our entire church family."

Ninety-five percent of Protestant churches (nineteen out of every twenty) still offer Sunday school "in which people receive some form of planned or systemic Bible instruction in a class setting."[10] That amounts to more than 300,000 churches and nearly 45 million adults and more than 22 million youth and children every weekend.[11] But only one in seven senior pastors (15 percent) considers Sunday school to be their church's highest priority. This represents a significant drop from previous years.

Most of the surveyed women told me they support, and even "cheer" small group Sunday school classes.

An Oregon woman writes: "Women need to be in interactive small groups for Bible study and prayer in order to grow in their relationship with God. Even the best sermon every week is not going to meet all their spiritual needs. Many women come to church under so much stress, and with so many distractions, they might only hear half the Sunday sermon."

"The greatest need of Christian women today," writes another, "is to be in a women's Bible study that offers prayer support and serious instruction in the Word."

Some women, however, admit their church has no Bible-based Sunday school program: "My church offers few opportunities for spiritual growth outside of Sunday church worship," responds one woman, who adds a plea: "Pastor, please provide opportunities for women to have solid Bible teaching on a weekly basis."

A Texas woman wants Sunday school classes that "help women to deeply and thoroughly know God and his Word, and to live out what they know. Both have to go together," she writes, and stresses that women need "good, trusted, deeply loving and nurturing discipleship."

A Florida woman suggests that spiritual maturity and similar interests—instead of age—be the deciding point for grouping women into Sunday school classes. "When Sunday school groups are segregated by age, it can create even more of a sense of aloneness," she writes.

Almost all the women surveyed consider Sunday school essential to the work of the church. The good news is: Sunday school seems alive and well in the church today.

GETTING SERIOUS ABOUT FAITH

God's Word tells a Christian woman to first love God with her whole heart, soul, mind and strength, and then to love her neighbor as herself (Matthew 22:37 – 39). When a pastor intentionally teaches scriptural truth and when he encourages women to spend time in personal Bible study and prayer, he arms them with the necessary equipment to reach out to other women with God's Word. They become eager evangelists, as well as theologians who can rightly interpret the Word, model it, and teach it to others. A spiritually mature woman, who knows her Scripture, can multiply immensely the church's ministry. She can take God's Word into places where Christian men might never be invited.

"Women are vital to the body of Christ," writes a New England woman. "We need ministry to evangelize women and nurture their Christian walk. This is foundational to the entire function of the body of Christ—the church. But," she adds, "sometimes I feel our pastors fail to see the significance of these roles [as evidenced by what's budgeted for women's needs and ministries]. Children, music, and youth ministries, to mention a few, get much attention. While those programs are certainly highly needed, we must also minister to the Christian mother who supports and nurtures those children and teens, and brings them to church in the first place. The bottom line: Women NEED ministry programs to evangelize, teach, encourage, and support women. This calls for budgeted dollars designated for women's ministries with targeted goals."

"The women I know crave small groups in the community and church that combine Bible study with outreach to the church, city, and world," says a woman from North Carolina. "Bible studies have multiplied in our church, and have created caring small groups that encourage one another to live out faith in a tangible way. At the same time, our women's groups that are centering on meeting needs outside the church walls are also growing in number, passion, and involvement. *Getting serious about faith is a fresh breath of the Spirit.*"

Today's Christian woman wants her pastor to know that:

- We live in a time of intense spiritual hunger. Women are looking for theological answers to life's deepest questions.
- Women want *serious* study of theology. They want spiritual "meat," not spiritual "milk."
- Women need God's truth from God's Word to survive the demands and hardships of everyday life.
- Scripture shows that Jesus respected the minds of women in his day, and he taught them deep spiritual doctrine.
- A Christian woman yearns to spend personal quiet time with God, but her devotional time is often limited due to constant pressing demands on her time and energy.
- Lack of quiet time spent with God and his Word leaves a Christian woman feeling frustrated, "off center," and unbalanced in every area of her life. She needs God's Word in the setting of both personal and corporate Bible study.
- The church is doing a good job teaching Scripture and theology through well-organized Sunday school programs.
- Women who are spiritually mature and theologically knowledgeable yearn to take God's Word and Christ's love into the spiritually dead world.

PART 3

THE FAMILY LIFE
OF WOMEN IN
YOUR CHURCH

CHAPTER 6

"PASTOR, I HAVE PROBLEMS IN MY MARRIAGE"

The sad truth is that home is where the greatest abuses in power and influence are committed against our most intimate relationships.[1]

Tim Kimmel

SOME CHRISTIAN WOMEN are called by God to remain single. I applaud these women who honor God's calling and live a life without marriage. This chapter, however, concerns the married woman who experiences serious problems in her marriage.

Research tells us that a woman in a healthy marriage prospers in numerous ways. Even her physical health is better. A study conducted by the University of Pittsburgh found that women in good marriages have a much lower risk of cardiovascular disease than those in high-stress relationships. The National Longitudinal Mortality Study, which has been tracking more than a million subjects since 1979, shows that married people live longer, have fewer heart attacks and lower cancer rates, and even get pneumonia less frequently than singles.[2]

In my three decades of ministry travels and speaking to large groups of Christian women, however, I have met few women who enjoy good, healthy marriages. The survey responses I received from hundreds of women also reveal this dilemma. Women today face numerous trials, trauma, and even desperation in their marriages. Many come from, and now live in, dysfunctional families—a "family in which alcoholism, drug abuse, divorce, absent father or mother, excessive anger, verbal and/or physical abuse exists."[3] We've already seen how a woman's nature is relational, and how women thrive when their relationships are satisfying, close, and healthy. Next to her relationship with Jesus Christ, a married woman's closest, most intimate relationship is with her husband. When her marriage is upset, or her family is dysfunctional, a woman's entire world turns upside down.

A New Mexico woman agrees: "Deep inside of me, my home (husband, family) is more important to me than my job (which happens to be in ministry at a church). If my home life feels scattered, I am most likely going to feel overwhelmed and disorganized at work. Even though I work outside the home, my home is still my number one priority."

A woman's marriage/home is her haven—her nest. Marriage is the relationship that promises to provide her love, trust, rest, enjoyment, affirmation, purpose, and fulfillment. It's the place—in her heart and her home—where she can "just be herself" without pretense or "show." Marriage is supposed to offer a woman security—physical, emotional, mental, spiritual, and financial. Most women want a husband they can look up to with love, appreciation, and admiration; someone they can communicate with deeply; a strong spiritual leader who loves the Lord and keeps the family focused on Christ. A woman wants to open her whole heart and soul to one human man, to be "at one" with him, to never fear his actions, decisions, or harsh words. She wants the "Cinderella" life she's been promised by fairy tales, media, and often, her parents. She yearns to find that "perfect" man and "live happily ever after."

NO PERFECT PARTNERS

However, by the end of the first year of marriage—or much sooner—most husbands and wives realize that neither husbands nor wives are "perfect people." All healthy marriages experience some problems. Usually these problems are communicated, faced, solved, and the marriage becomes stronger and more committed to survive. But Christian women today are experiencing serious trauma in their marriages. Many suffer on a daily basis. Their problems aren't being communicated, faced, and solved, but are growing worse, and are steadily weakening the marriage. Some marital dilemmas can even be life threatening to a woman.

I want to introduce you to seven women in your church. Believe it or not, the problems these women deal with are common ones. Most of these women will suffer in silence because they are embarrassed and ashamed.

They keep silent because of fear, or because they don't want to damage a husband's position or standing in the church and community. Few in the church will know the deep pain marriage brings for each of them. But these women need help from their pastor and their church.

Meet Janice, a Victim of Divorce

This year Janice celebrated her sixtieth birthday, and her husband of forty years divorced her. He found a younger woman and plans to marry her. Janice is emotionally crushed. She feels rejected and unloved, like her life has gone "down the drain." Since the divorce, many of the couple's mutual friends haven't stayed in touch.

But Janice's pastor and church reached out to her. They showed her their love, arranged for her to receive Christian counseling, involved her fully in the women's ministry program, educated her about various community divorce support groups, and ministered to her with practical help. They helped her get on her feet emotionally. Janice recovered, and today she is active in church, thriving in life, and growing spiritually.

Some of the women I surveyed, however, voiced a far different reaction from the church. A newly divorced mother with two teenagers writes:

> I'm upset about the different treatment women get, and go through, in the two ways they can become single moms. One way is the death of a spouse. A widow is instantly surrounded with love, friendship, lots of food, extreme amounts of prayer, continuous follow-up, and sympathy from church members. The widow is treated special, and usually included in events by everyone. Becoming a widow is considered okay in our church and society.
>
> Then there are those of us whose husbands wanted more affairs than they could count, and who chose another family altogether, and created a "new life" (for the wife) called "single mom." These divorced/abandoned women are "not okay" in society because we are divorced. We do not get love, dinners, sympathy, continuous follow-up. Instead we are ostracized. Church people ignore us, because they don't know what to say to a newly divorced woman. So, divorced women sit alone in church. Other church wives may wonder why their husbands are talking to the church's divorced women.
>
> Often, ministers don't know what to say either. Men and ministers can't take the chance of being seen talking with a divorced woman. They are, however, comfortable talking to a widow. You see, the one—the widow—is loved by the church and is

surrounded with pastoral Christian fellowship. The other—the divorced woman—is "out" as far as church and society go. And what's so sad is this: both women lost their husband and need the love and support of the church.

A divorced woman from Georgia—a hardworking, faithful, twenty-year member of her church—had a similar experience. She writes:

> After twenty-one years of marriage, my alcoholic husband divorced me. I was single for three years, and then I married a man I met at church. He was sexually unfaithful, and we divorced after seven rocky years of marriage. For five years after that, I stayed single. Then I married another man from my church. He walked out after two years of marriage because "he didn't think he wanted to be married."
>
> I now have a "brand" on my forehead—put there by my fellow church members. Many of the members of my church are very narrow-minded about divorced women. Had I been a widow, I believe it would've been a different story. At my church, they "take care" of their widows. But divorced women? Forget it!
>
> When my husband walked out on me two years ago, I really didn't expect anything from anyone in my church even though I was an active church member. (I was a choir member, worked in children's church, and served on the stewardship committee. I often sang solos in church, as well as played the piano, saxophone, and organ.) My pastor has yet to ask how I am doing since my divorce.
>
> What do I wish my pastor knew? That divorced women have the same feelings of loneliness that a widow has. We go through periods of grief too. Divorce happens, and it happens to good people! We really aren't "bad people," and God loves us just as much as he loves those fine married people who smile and say they have "happy" marriages!

Sometimes divorced Christian women can feel like spiritual failures. They know that God hates divorce (Malachi 2:16), and wonder if he can still use them in his kingdom work after a failed marriage. Whenever a divorced Christian woman asks me this question, I tell her the story of Jesus' purposeful encounter at Jacob's well with a divorced Samaritan woman (John 4). Jesus met her at the noon hour, the hottest time of the day. She had chosen that inopportune time in order to avoid the gossip and looks of disgust from the married women who drew their water in the cool, early hours.

During the conversation, Jesus asked her to "go, call your husband and come back" (4:16). She admitted to him that she had no husband. In fact, Jesus, in his omniscience, told her, she had already been divorced five times and was now living with another man.

But did he reject her? No. Instead he filled her heart with Living Water, and appointed her as his missionary to Samaria. Did she do the work Jesus gave her to do? Yes. "Many of the Samaritans from that town believed in him because of the woman's testimony" (4:39).

Meet Joyce, a Victim of Physical Spouse Abuse

Joyce, a middle-aged woman with grown children, has spent her life as a stay-at-home mother and full-time homemaker. The children are grown and gone now. No one at church knows that Joyce is a victim of spouse abuse. Her husband beats her to control her. He has almost destroyed Joyce's body and soul. Sad and timid, she has long ago lost her sense of self.

No doubt, you already know some general statistics on physical spouse abuse, but consider these specifics: Up to 6 million women are believed to be beaten in their homes each year. Four million incidents are reported. Up to 90 percent of battered women never report their abuse. On the average, a woman is battered in the United States by a partner every twelve to fifteen seconds! Fifty percent of all homeless women and children in America are fleeing domestic violence. Fifty to 70 percent of men who abuse their partners also abuse children in the home. The average batterer is held less than two hours, and less than 1 percent serve any jail time.[4]

Have you ever wondered why Joyce wears such heavy makeup? She is hiding black eyes and bruises. She also wears heavy clothes that cover the bruises on her arms and legs, even in the summer. Joyce risks setting off her husband's temper every time she comes to church. Yet she so desperately needs a word from God, she risks the abuse and attends the worship services. Joyce doesn't come to the church's other activities though. Her husband won't allow her to.

"I know of so many women who have been battered, bruised, abused, heartbroken, betrayed, and [suffered] so many other travesties," writes a woman from Colorado. "They come to church looking for help."

Domestic abuse knows no boundaries. Educational background, income, class, race, or faith seem to make little difference. Society has long known about spouse abuse, but fear, embarrassment, and practical concerns cover it with a blanket of silence.

Spouse abuse shocks us. We just cannot believe that a church deacon or member goes home after worship services and physically hurts/beats his wife. A therapist writes: "In my early years as a therapist, I was surprised and saddened that many of the perpetrators of sexual abuse and domestic violence I counseled professed to be Christians. I was particularly confused by the many perpetrators who claimed to see no conflict between their behavior and their Christian beliefs. Some even justified their behavior by citing biblical passages and religious principles. For several years I was baffled. How could people who professed to be devout Christians do such un-Christlike things to others?"[5]

Domestic violence has become an epidemic in the United States. Yet few churches know how to deal with it.

One survey asked 5,700 pastors how they would counsel a woman who was the target of spousal abuse. Here's how they answered:

- 26 percent would counsel a woman to continue to submit,
- 25 percent said the wife's failure to submit was the cause of the abuse in the first place,
- 50 percent said women should tolerate some level of violence in the home because to do so is better than divorce,
- 71 percent said they would never counsel a battered wife to leave her husband,
- 92 percent said they would never suggest divorce.[6]

When pastors counsel abused church women in this way, their advice often puts these women in grave danger. However well-intentioned, telling a wife to return to her abusive husband may be issuing her a death warrant. Over 30 percent (some estimate over 50 percent) of all murders of women in America are committed by intimate partners.[7] When deaths from such violence occur, in 85 to 90 percent of the cases police had been called to the home for domestic violence at least once during the two years before the killing; in more than half the cases, police had been called five or more times. Often when the woman reports the case to police, the attacker becomes more violent.[8]

In the book *Women, Abuse, and the Bible*, Carolyn Holderread Heggen writes about a pastor who told an abused woman: "'No matter what he's doing to you, he is still your spiritual head. Respect those behaviors that you can respect and pray for those that you can't respect. But remember, no matter what, you owe it to him and to God to live in submission to your husband. You'll never be happy until you submit to him.'"[9]

Again, this is dangerous advice. The word *submit* can be so misinterpreted that, in some cases, abusive husbands may be wrongly convinced that Paul's words actually give them permission to physically abuse a wife.

Pastors also make a huge mistake when they counsel an abusive husband and his wife together. The wife is afraid to speak, and if she does, she risks further abuse from her husband when they return home.

What should a pastor do when he discovers spouse abuse in his church? He must intervene. The physical abuse cannot continue. The abuse will not stop on its own. It will accelerate. Until her husband can receive the treatment he needs, the abused woman and her children must be removed from the situation. The wise pastor will have a list of Christian counselors to help her, as well as information about a safe house where she and her children can go for safety.

Thankfully, I see more and more pastors opening their eyes to the problem of spouse abuse in the church. I especially appreciate the stand taken by Pastor Frank A. Thomas, when he preached a sermon in his church on domestic violence. His words include these:

> After much study, prayer, and reflection, I have come to an important position in regards to abuse and domestic violence. I do not have to be right, and I know that there are some of you that might disagree with me, but I want to make sure my position is clear. I do not believe that it is God's will for any person to stay in a violent and abusive relationship under the justification that God does not condone divorce. I am not advocating divorce, or an easy exit from the lifelong commitment of marriage, but I believe that God does not desire that anyone subject themselves to abuse and violence. I do not believe that God requires any spouse to be beaten as a part of the marriage covenant. Therefore, if someone is abusive, then the victim of the crime by all means has the right to leave.[10]

Steven R. Fleming, in "Competent Christian Intervention with Men Who Batter," writes about domestic violence and a pastor's response to it: "Church leaders can be part of the problem or choose to be part of the solution. To be part of the solution, leaders can preach about domestic violence from the pulpit. If done with care and sensitivity, this will raise awareness of the problem and let the perpetrator sitting in the pew know that violence is immoral and will not be tolerated."[11]

For more information about spouse abuse problems in your church, I'd recommend Steven R. Tracy's book, *Mending the Soul: Understanding and*

Healing Abuse (Zondervan, 2005). Tracy includes five helpful appendices with worksheets pastors can photocopy.

Meet Miriam, a Victim of Emotional and Verbal Spouse Abuse

Domestic violence and spouse abuse come in many forms. Joyce was the victim of physical battering. Miriam's husband, on the other hand, doesn't hit or beat her, but his emotional and verbal abuse hurt just as much. Women tell me that emotional abuse scars their hearts and minds, while physical abuse scars their bodies. With physical abuse, women have the proof of black eyes and bruises to validate their experiences. But victims of emotional and verbal abuse often place blame on themselves, not on their husband. They are reluctant to consider themselves abused women.

Miriam's husband humiliates her in front of her friends. He controls her every move through intimidating manipulation. He holds tight the financial purse strings, and often threatens her with divorce and loss of all income. He keeps her isolated from friends and family members, monitors her phone calls, and usually keeps her from attending church worship and other church activities. Miriam often feels like a prisoner in her own home.

Her husband calls her names, tells her she is stupid and worthless, and accuses her of unfaithfulness. So beaten down emotionally, Miriam endures his profanity and demeaning insults.

"Cruelty is generally thought of in terms of physical pain," writes Karl Menninger. "But there is a kind of personal injury, given and taken, which is not physically but psychologically painful, and which may also be economically and socially damaging. I refer to the use of words as weapons.... Hurled from the hoarse throat of a more powerful figure, accompanied by threats of injury, reinforced by angry facial contortions and physical gestures, name-calling and cursing can become cruelly painful."[12]

Like Joyce, Miriam is deeply hurting. She might never tell her pastor face-to-face, but she desperately needs his help.

I received many surveys from women whose husbands hurt them and controlled them through emotional and verbal abuse. The women spoke about "constant stomachaches" when their husband was in the house, and about "walking on eggshells" to keep from upsetting him. Most told me they struggled with fear from day to day. Some were receiving help from Christian pastors and counselors. But many more suffered in silence, and prayed the problem would go away.

Meet Sheila, Whose Husband Has a "Dirty Little Secret"

Sheila's husband is one of the many Christians in this country who is secretly addicted to something that causes him shame and self-destruction. Christian husbands today may have addictions to sex, pornography, drugs, alcohol, and other things that stay hidden within the walls of a home. Sheila's husband's addiction is pornography. After Sunday morning worship services — as well as after work each day — he disappears into his study, turns on his computer, and stays mesmerized with websites that produce degrading and disgraceful pornographic images. Sheila keeps his shameful behavior a secret. But she is filled with shame and hate for his "dirty little secret." And she doesn't know what to do about it.

Dr. Mark Laaser, director of Faithful and True Ministries, an organization that counsels Christians struggling with sexual sin, says "web porn may become the number one problem facing the church in the next few years."

"It's an epidemic," says Laaser. "People are getting addicted to it. All the classic signs of addiction apply. They get totally out of control."[13]

Statistics show that "40 million Americans regularly view Internet pornography, which accounts for $2.5 billion of the $12 billion U.S. porn industry."[14]

Some professionals believe that Christians turn to pornography because they are looking for intimacy. For whatever reason, the addiction affects one in five people in the pews.[15] Others say porn addictions come from emotional pain — from childhood abuse, from feeling isolated, rejected, or inadequate — [and are] compounded by not having someone to talk with about it.

Pornography is not just about sex," writes psychologist Dr. Simon Sheh. "It is a drug of pain relief." Dr. Sheh believes that "recognizing those factors helps men deal with the shame of seeking help."[16]

Listen to the pain expressed by one wife whose husband had an addiction to porn. She writes: "I'm a wife. I'm a wife of a porn addict. I'm relieved to know what it is, though I always knew something was wrong. Tears. Pain. Disgust. Betrayal. To face the death of a husband would be better than this. A widow has the support of the church. A porn addict leaves shame and divorce. It would be easier if he were dead. We wouldn't have to face the public humiliation and shame."[17]

A number of the survey responses indicate that Christian women are dealing with a husband's secret addiction to "cyberporn."

A Texas woman keeps her husband's cybersex a secret, but writes: "Women wish the church really knew their husbands. They put these men in godly church positions, and they are not always what they appear to be."

"Women are embarrassed to go to their pastor about a husband's sexual addictions," writes another wife. "Many Christian women want to protect their children from embarrassment, so they keep things hidden."

A Minnesota wife writes: "Pornography is not just a man's problem. A husband's dalliance in or addiction to Internet pornography has a devastating effect on his wife. Women suffer through this insidious attack on their marriages most often in silence, shame, and guilt."

Many women told me they had personally dealt with a husband's sexual pornography addictions. They blamed their husbands for choosing online porn over spending time with their family. They resented their husband's preoccupation with distasteful sexual images and fantasies. But, to my surprise, one woman blamed the wives themselves for their husband's pornographic habits. She wrote: "So many men/husbands deal with pornography. I think if we as wives take our roles seriously, and seek to honor and bless our husbands (instead of trying to be self-fulfilled women), then the incidence of pornography use among married Christian men would decline."

In my own research, and in talking with numerous professionals, I have yet to discover any evidence that supports this woman's view.

"Online porn gives my husband private and easy access to every type of porn imaginable. He no longer has to walk into a seedy bookstore and purchase it. Porn is readily available to him at the touch of a button, and it's fairly inexpensive," writes another woman.

"Online porn has attracted a surprising number of married, professional men. Most of them have never had a problem with porn before.... For some, curiosity has progressed to obsession.... And the need grows. They require more and more to keep from getting bored."[18]

Internet pornography has earned itself a reputation for being the "crack cocaine of sexual addiction ... [it] works so quickly and it's so instantly intense," says Dr. Robert Weiss of the Sexual Recovery Institute in Los Angeles.[19]

As already mentioned, a husband's Internet porn addiction hurts the entire family. His preoccupation with computer sexual images keeps him from interacting fully with his wife and children. All addictions lead to the spiritual, emotional, physical, and social destruction of the addict, who most often will experience guilt, embarrassment, self-hatred, and shame.

Unless he gets help, his addictions can lead to more self-destructive behavior. Cybersex addictions can quickly destroy a marriage, shame a family, break a wife's heart, and lead to a painful divorce.

Women in the church are mostly suffering in silence, but they want their pastors to know that they as wives deal with hurt, grief, embarrassment, and shame because of a husband's sexual addictions, infidelity, and addictions to pornography, drugs, and alcohol. They want help, but they don't know how to ask for it.

Meet Sydney, Whose Husband Is Homosexual

A number of women wrote to me about a Christian husband's secret homosexuality. Sydney told me she was married for almost twenty years before she discovered her husband and father of her two teenaged children lived a double life and had a homosexual lover. To the church and community, he seemed a deeply spiritual, outgoing, and charming husband and father. He held positions of leadership in their church. No one had a clue that he had had a decade long sexual relationship with another man.

Sydney finally learned of her husband's homosexuality when he became extremely ill after contracting AIDS and was forced to tell her his secret.

"When I heard the news, I felt like I had been kicked in the stomach," Sydney admitted. "I never suspected a thing! For a long time, I walked around in shock. I was devastated."

Sydney and her husband divorced, and he eventually died from the disease.

What is homosexuality? Author Lawrence J. Hatterer gives this definition: "One who is motivated, in adult life, by a definite preferential erotic attraction to members of the same sex and who usually, but not necessarily, engages in overt sexual relations with them."[20]

Homosexuality proves a complex problem for the church today. And it's not just a man's problem. One woman from Michigan writes: "Women in my church struggle with lesbianism just as often as men struggle with homosexuality."

Another writes: "Homosexuality is ruining the lives of many of our church's young people—mostly males, but females too. Homosexuality is destroying even Christian families, because of its hold on many adult men, yes even married men, and even some married women."

While a woman is usually quiet about a husband's homosexuality, she inwardly yearns for her pastor to know and to offer help.

Meet Nicole, a Financially Hurting Married Woman

Financial debt and bankruptcy can quickly end a Christian marriage. Nicole's husband, Tom, has poor money-managing skills. Both work full time to keep bread on the table and a roof over their family's heads.

Without considering Nicole's involvement, Tom might splurge on a new car or boat, impulsively spending large amounts of money they don't have. His credit card spending has put the family in deep financial trouble. On the outside, Nicole and Tom seem healthy, but behind closed doors, they constantly argue and fight about Tom's uncontrollable spending. If financial relief doesn't come soon, the couple will be forced to file for bankruptcy.

In an article, "The Emotional Toll of Bankruptcy," Harvard Law School professor Elizabeth Warren explains that the "main three reasons for filing [bankruptcy] are job loss, medical [issues], and family breakup. These three reasons account for about 90 percent of all filings," she says, "with many debtors hit by two or even all three events."[21]

Unexpected job loss, high medical bills, and family breakup are often factors that can't be anticipated or controlled. But Tom's spending habits are voluntary. The damage, however, is the same.

Untamed spending habits, unlimited credit possibilities, and "easy cash" can quickly devastate a family's paycheck. The total debt outstanding among Americans has doubled in the past decade to more than two trillion dollars! "American consumers wouldn't be as deeply in debt ... without the active encouragement of a lending industry that is hauling in billions in profits on all that interest."[22]

I have been amazed at the proliferation of credit card offers addressed to our daughter that daily fill our mailbox. Never mind that our daughter is a full-time, non-income-earning, parental-supported college student with limited funds! With what looks like "easy money," credit cards can put America's young people in great financial straits before they even get their first job! They enter the work force already enslaved by debt.

American consumers are filing for bankruptcy in record numbers. As financial debt increases, churches will see more marriages end in divorce. Or worse! In an article, "Pathological Consumption," Addison Wiggin writes about a call he received from the *Boston Herald*. "The reporter told me there was a horrific murder in his city ... the alleged murderer, Neil Entwistle, ostensibly killed his wife and nine-month-old son because he was up to his eyeballs in debt."

Wiggin found out that Entwistle carried $8,000 in credit card debt (the national average is $9,312), and owed another $25,000 in student loans. His monthly rent was $2,700 on a $375,000 house.[23]

What does financial debt and bankruptcy do to a husband and wife? It can upset a family in the same way as a death or a divorce. Many families grieve the action and loss for years.

Nicole is ashamed of her family's need to file bankruptcy. She wants her pastor to know that she has struggled hard to maintain good credit, to tithe 10 percent of the family income, and to keep her family financially afloat. But her husband's uncontrollable spending habits have undermined her effort. She also wants her pastor to know that financial debt has greatly hurt their relationship, and, unless her husband gets help with his spending problem, she is sure the marriage won't last.

Meet Nellie, a Financially Hurting Divorced Woman

Nellie has a financial problem just as severe as Nicole's, but much different. Nellie and her husband of thirty-five years, Mike, always maintained good credit ratings, paid their bills on time, and managed to put some money into a savings account. Money was never an issue that caused them marital distress. Mike made an adequate salary, and Nellie chose to work as a full-time homemaker and mother. They were careful not to overspend, but made sure the family had daily necessities.

Nellie's financial problems came when Mike, without good reason, divorced her. Divorce both shocked and hurt Nellie, as well as devastating her financially. For the first time since her wedding, Nellie had to search for a job. Nellie's premarriage secretarial skills were rusty. With the coming of computers, she felt "left behind" in the job market. At the time of her divorce, Nellie's financial resources dropped by more than half. She had no medical or life insurance, or retirement plan. She could barely survive on what little money she received each month.

Did you know that, for the first time in history, more married women will become single due to divorce than due to a husband's death?

"Until recently, women alone generally meant widows, who at least had the pensions and savings their husbands had left them, and a tradition of living with children. Widows greatly outnumbered older divorced women until the late 1990s, but now for the first time the divorced outnumber widows."[24]

Most of these women will suffer a severe financial setback, and will be walking the city streets looking for jobs. For many, retirement will be impossible.

"Divorce is responsible for the scores of older women who must go back to work in order to financially support themselves," writes Louis Uchitelle, in a recent *New York Times* article. "Hundreds of thousands of women in their 60s, part of the surge of divorces that started a generation ago, are finding themselves forced to stay in the work force because they lack sufficient money to retire. Wages in effect are becoming their pensions."[25]

Women like Nellie need the church's prayer support. They might also need financial help from the church.

TEACH MEN HOW TO LOVE THEIR WIVES

No husband can meet all of his wife's physical, emotional, mental, and spiritual needs. A woman who expects that impossible task from her husband will be disappointed. She will also be prone to smother him, be too demanding of his time and energy, and end up frustrated and perhaps alone. But women want their pastors to help educate men to be better husbands. They want the church to teach men how to love their wives, and commit themselves wholly to their marriages. They want their husbands to take Scripture seriously when Paul tells them to love their wives as Christ loved the church (Christ loved the church so much that he gave his life for her); to love their wives as their own bodies (care for her with special tenderness and nurture); and to love their wives as they love themselves (show them respect, concern, and loyalty).

Most of the surveys stated emphatically that women desire to "submit to [their] husbands as to the Lord" (Ephesians 5:22). They take to heart Paul's words: "For the husband is the head of the wife as Christ is the head of the church, his body, of which he is the Savior. Now as the church submits to Christ, so also wives should submit to their husbands in everything" (5:23–24).

The problem comes, however, when a husband doesn't love his wife as Christ loved the church. As we have already seen, some husbands abuse their wives and children, desert and divorce their families, compromise their marriage with secret addictions, and refuse to spiritually lead their homes.

One woman writes: "I wish pastors truly understood that submission comes easily to Christian women who see their husbands submitting to the leadership of the Holy Spirit, and follow without compromise where God leads him. I believe a godly woman understands God's design for the line of authority and is grateful for his protection."

A pastor can be instrumental in helping husbands understand the basic needs of every wife. Some men don't have a clue how different women's needs are from the needs of men. Today's Christian woman wants her husband to

- love and respect her, and show it tangibly;
- be the strong spiritual leader of their home;
- be trustworthy himself, and trust her as well;
- be concerned about her physical, emotional, mental, and spiritual well-being;
- make her feel physically and emotionally safe;
- help provide for her financially;
- listen to her with attention and understanding when she needs to talk;
- affirm, encourage, and praise her;
- touch her lovingly, but in nonsexual ways;
- passionately desire her in sexual ways;
- help her in practical ways at home—with work and children;
- include her in his thoughts, dreams, and activities;
- be kind, considerate, and giving.

The pastor and church who seek to teach their men the art of being good husbands strengthen marriages and families, and, in doing so, build up the entire church body.

Not long ago in a church worship service, a married couple sat behind me, and I heard the woman quietly pray: "Thank you, Lord, for my marriage, and for this wonderful husband."

At the time, I thought to myself: *How I wish every Christian woman could honestly pray those words!*

A "SAFE" PERSON TO TALK WITH

While some women desire to keep their personal lives private, many more wish their pastors knew the difficulties they face. Why? The Christian woman whose marriage is in turmoil knows her pastor is a "safe" person to talk with. She trusts him to keep shared information confidential. She knows he has the authority and power to do something about her problems. (This is especially true in cases of spouse abuse and various addictions), and that he will listen to her, validate her, and advise her in biblical ways.

Because he has encountered the same or similar situations in the church, she realizes he is likely networked to resources within the church and community to help her and her family. She also knows that a pastor can professionally confront a husband who needs confronting, and that her husband will more than likely respect his pastoral authority.

SURVEY SUMMARY

Today's Christian woman wants her pastor to know that:

- Other than God, her husband is her closest, most intimate relationship.
- She often experiences pain and frustration in her marriage.
- When she and her husband are having problems, her entire world is upset.
- Divorce devastates her, and, like the widow who has lost a husband, she too needs the church's special love, concern, support, and fellowship.
- Her divorce doesn't mean she is a spiritual failure; God can still use her in his work.
- Spouse abuse in the Christian home is common these days, and it is destroying her body and soul. She desperately needs intervention and help.
- Her husband brings his "dirty little secrets" into their home, and she is helplessly watching him destroy himself and his family.
- She is hurting financially and doesn't know what to do.
- She desperately wants a Christian marriage.
- She yearns for her husband to love her like Christ loves the church.
- She needs help to make Christ the center of her marriage and home.

"PASTOR, MY CHILDREN ARE IMPORTANT TO ME"

Almighty God, Our Heavenly Parent,

You have entrusted to us a life so fragile, so vulnerable, so completely dependent. We are afraid. How can we bear so weighty a responsibility? What if we make an uncorrectable mistake? What if we love too leniently or discipline too severely? What if ... Free us from the fear of failure.

Teach us that parenthood does not come like a cake mix—in four easy steps. Only in the daily doing of it will we learn the proper balance. Give us the grace to be good hosts. Remind us that this little one who will walk beside us for a few short years is only a guest in our home. We have no ironclad claims to his soul, body or life. Let us offer hospitality and kindness, gentle nudges and loving hands to mend the hurts.

Sustain us in the storms of life. When we have reached our limit, when the world has done its worst, help us to say "Into thy hands, O Lord, we commit it all." In life, in death, today and every tomorrow, O thou who stillest raging winds, be near. Through Jesus Christ who was once a little baby, Amen.[1]

Timothy George

CHRISTIAN PARENTS OFTEN STRUGGLE to raise godly children. These days, society doesn't teach or promote godliness. When they bring children into this world, most women are keenly aware of their new responsibilities—physical, emotional, mental, financial, and spiritual. Often, a mother must take on all these responsibilities alone, especially if she is single, divorced, abandoned, or widowed. Sometimes, due to an ill, irresponsible, or unconcerned husband, even a married woman must parent alone. Nowadays, many more grandmothers are taking on the full-time care of their grandchildren. They raise their own children, empty the nest, and then, as retirement approaches, they refill their nests with their children's children. Regardless of a mother's situation in life, she often turns to the church for encouragement, support, and practical help with the exhausting job of Christian mothering.

A MOM'S NUMBER ONE PRIORITY

Christian mothers tell me "children are a woman's number one priority!" "We all want to know how to raise godly children in an increasingly secular society," a Wisconsin mother writes. They also admit "nothing about child rearing is easy these days." Christian moms realize "all of our children are unique gifts from God. We need to cherish each child with obvious love and affection, recognizing each child's unique personality, individual capabilities, and special needs."[2]

They truly want the best for their "unique gifts from God," but they sometimes feel like "Lone Ranger moms" trying singlehandedly to raise godly children in a godless society.

"I'm swimming upstream," a mother with three youngsters writes. "I'm struggling to rear my three little girls to one day become Christ-centered women. Everywhere I turn, however, society seems to be working against me. I need the church's help like never before!"

A Christian grandmother from Missouri writes: "Mothers need help and encouragement in raising the next generation of Christians. How important it is for women to make sure the next generation of children know Christ and grow as Christians."

THE URGENCY OF A CHILD'S SALVATION

I hear Christian moms state with firm conviction the urgency of their children's salvation in Jesus Christ and the importance of their children's spiritual upbringing. That's why a recent parenting study by George Barna surprises me. His research shows that "born again" parents today do not consider a child's salvation through Jesus Christ to be one of their most critical parental emphases! Barna's findings also surprised him. He writes: "One of the most startling observations . . . was how few born again parents indicated that one of the most important outcomes parents needed to help their children grasp was salvation through faith in Jesus Christ. Only three out of ten born again parents included the salvation of their child in the list of critical parental emphases."

But Barna adds: "For years we have reported research findings showing that born again adults think and behave very much like everyone else. It often seems that their faith makes very little difference in their life. This new study helps explain why that is: believers do not train their children to think or act any differently."[3]

If this recent study truly represents the hearts and minds of Christian parents today, pastors and churches need to firmly step into the lives of parents and change this growing trend. Never has the church been needed more than today to help parents raise godly children!

SOME OBSTACLES TO CHRISTIAN MOTHERING

Mothers today face a number of obstacles. We've already seen how exhaustion, stress, and hurtful life situations have taken a toll on moms. Each pastor must recognize the difficult situations today's Christian moms experience and strive to address each of them. While some hardships are common to all mothers, let's consider for a moment the unique needs of the Christian mother who is:

A Single Mom

Whether never married, divorced, or widowed, the single mom is often on her own to supply all her child's needs. Typically this means she must work long hours both inside and outside the home. Single moms often feel guilty because they can't spend more time with their children.

"Our worry about our children getting enough time with us causes many mothers to create time for them by giving up on time for themselves. Whether it's a decrease in sleep, hobbies, or a social life, women, more than men, pay for time by decreasing the amount spent on other personal needs and interests."

One mother admits: "I just feel so selfish taking time for myself. It isn't even that I want to spend every waking second with them. It's more like I feel like if I don't, it means I'm a terrible mother."[4]

Single mothers tell me they pray someone in the church will offer to help them with some practical needs. They just simply can't do everything without help! The congregation might consider a special ministry to single moms, supporting them with encouragement, prayer, and practical assistance in their everyday lives.

A New Mom

Whether teenaged or middle aged, a mother with a new baby needs help! This is especially true if she lives far away from her extended family. A new baby most often turns a woman's world upside down and brings tremendous challenges and chaos. I personally waited eleven years before I gave birth to my first child. When my son, Christian, was born, I was closer to middle age than teenage.

After his birth, I quickly discovered that life was a whole new ballgame. Neither Timothy nor I had had any experience with babies. In fact, neither one of us had ever changed a diaper! When we brought three-day-old Christian home from the hospital, we honestly didn't know which end of him to take care of first. Should we feed him? Or change him? Earlier we had laughed when other new parents jokingly told us their definition of a baby: "A ravenous appetite at one end, and complete irresponsibility at the other end." But we weren't laughing now! We were completely overwhelmed with the responsibility that had suddenly become ours. We had a newborn baby who depended on us for his very life. When he got hungry, he screamed. When he wet his diapers, he fussed. He slept all day and kept us awake all night. He always wanted his own way, and he usually got it! I remember asking Timothy several times during those first few exhausting, confusing weeks: "Now just what were those reasons that you and I wanted children?" Those proved long days, and even longer nights. And our extended family members lived hundreds of miles away. We were totally on our own, and we were scared.

The church can have a powerful ministry to the new mom in the congregation. I believe every new mother needs a Titus 2 woman in her life — a mature Christian woman who has raised Christian children and "survived" the experience!

A Working Mom and a Stay-at-Home Mom

A woman can make no better investment than "to devote her time to the shaping of a precious child God has entrusted to her care. Nevertheless, motherhood is a challenging task that is often unappreciated and misunderstood in our society. Just as full-time moms can feel devalued by women employed outside the home, mothers who are forced to work for financial reasons often feel guilty for leaving their children in daycare. It's important for women to realize that, regardless of other responsibilities or occupations they maintain, the type of love, guidance, and influence they provide to their children is distinct and invaluable. Motherhood is a high calling, rich with rewards that are both earthly and eternal."[5]

While most Christian mothers today work at jobs outside the home, some still choose to be full-time stay-at-home moms.[6]

While both types of mothers may complain about concerns regarding their jobs, not to mention the exhaustion and stress, the mom who works outside the home usually comes in contact with other people. But the full-time stay-at-home mom can feel quite isolated. This is especially true when she also homeschools her children or when her extended family lives a distance away.

It's important for these mothers to stay in touch with other mothers as well as the outside world. The church can help these moms to network with other women through church activities, Bible study groups, and supportive programs such as MOPS (Mothers of Preschoolers).

"I am involved in a ministry for mothers of preschoolers called MOPS," an Alabama mother writes. "It is a wonderful ministry. It helps me to be a better mom through the fellowship and encouragement of the ministry."[7]

A Grandmother Raising Her Grandchildren Full Time

In the United States today, 4.5 million children (6 percent of our nation's children) live with their grandparents[8] — a 76 percent increase since 1970.[9] Some live with both grandparents, while others live with a lone grandmother. Researchers, public policy makers, and the media first began to notice the huge increases in grandparent maintained households around 1990. Research showed several reasons for this trend, including: increased drug abuse among parents, teen pregnancy, divorce, the rapid rise of single parent households, mental and physical illnesses, AIDS, crime, child abuse and neglect, and incarceration.[10]

While a grandparent's godly influence can be a valuable asset, research shows that grandparents raising grandchildren have poorer health, higher rates of clinical depression, and more chronic health problems than grandparents in more traditional roles.[11] Most grandparents rearing grandchildren are between the ages of fifty-five and sixty-four, and almost 25 percent are over age sixty-five. Most are poor. Some must begin new jobs after retirement to bear increased financial burdens. Others must leave their jobs to provide childcare for their grandchildren. Grandparents who live in senior housing complexes might be forced to move.[12]

Just imagine the many ways a congregation can minister to a grandmother raising grandchildren full time!

A Christian Mom Married to a Nonbeliever

When a Christian mom is married to an unbelieving husband, she must usually singlehandedly take responsibility for her children's spiritual education and church involvement. When you ask today's non-Christian dads about church, a lot of them give answers like computer genius Bill Gates—husband of Melinda, and father of Jennifer.

"Melinda is Catholic, goes to church, and wants to raise Jennifer that way," Gates states. "But [Melinda] offered me a deal. If I start going to church—my family was Congregationalist—then Jennifer could be raised in whatever religion I choose."

Gates admits that he is tempted, because he would prefer she have a religion that "has less theology and all" than Catholicism, but he has not yet taken up the offer.

"Just in terms of allocation of time resources, religion is not very efficient," he explains. "There's a lot more I could be doing on a Sunday morning."[13]

I received a long letter from a woman named Amanda, whose unbelieving husband not only refuses to attend church but openly (and loudly) balks at her church attendance. He insists that she not "indoctrinate" the children with her "fairy tales" religion, and tells her and the boys, "Church is for wimps!"

Amanda, a dedicated Christian, calls herself a "church widow." Speaking on behalf of Christian wives and mothers everywhere, she writes:

> They call us "church widows." We are the women who come to church every week without husbands, and, because of a husband's interference, often without our children. Many of us, in our commonality, feel alone in our struggles. We are often prevented, or discouraged, from teaching God's Word to our children. What should we do? Disregard our husband's desires not to teach them? Or teach the children behind his back? How can we keep from sharing our Christian beliefs with those we most love? How can we teach our children about morality, or integrity, or justice, or self-image without talking about God?
>
> As a Christian woman, I rely on the Lord to give my husband the headship and wisdom to spiritually lead our family. But he refuses. And as a nonbeliever, he isn't subject to the discipline of the church. I also feel hesitant to join in church activities created for church families, since my own family refuses to come. Sometimes I feel I am not taken as seriously by my church because I don't have the support of my husband in the church. And I often

incur the wrath of my husband and children for the time I spend at church and away from them. How I yearn for their support and encouragement—instead of their criticism—in my commitment to serve God.

David Murrow writes that "at least one-fifth of married women regularly worship without their husbands."[14]

Women with nonbelieving husbands pray that someone on the church staff or in the congregation will reach out to their husbands. "Unfortunately," writes a Georgia woman, "many women will wait a long time for such a male church leader. She may become discouraged and move on to another fellowship. Many of these women have much to offer the church body, but they aren't recognized because they are married to unbelieving, unchurched husbands."

Another writes: "Most church women I know are desperately trying to keep their families together. Families today do not have Christian husbands and fathers as their spiritual leaders. It's usually left up to the wife. As a result, our homes are crumbling."

Christian women married to non-Christian husbands complain about having to take charge of the spiritual leadership in the home.

"As a woman of God," writes an Arkansas wife, "I am left to take on the biblical role of the husband as the spiritual leader of the family. I've become the 'head of my household,' not by choice, but by necessity."

A Texas woman wants her pastor to know that "many women have to be the spiritual leaders in their homes because their partners are nonbelievers and are against going to church. Some husbands are professed sinners, and seem intent on staying that way. A mother cannot let her children be ignorant of the Word of God, so she is responsible for teaching them spiritually."

As the church, we have a wonderful opportunity to help and encourage the Amandas, Melindas, and others in our congregations. By presenting the gospel to nonbelieving husbands, leading them to Christ, and mentoring them in the faith, we can help Christian wives, mothers, and children experience Christ's transforming power in their family's lives.

A Christian Mother Married to a Non-Church-Participating Christian Husband

Sometimes the "church widow" is married to a *Christian* husband who refuses to spiritually lead his family or attend the local church. These mothers, just like the Amandas in our congregations, must also become the spiritual heads of their homes.

"My husband walked the church aisle and gave his heart to Christ as a teenager," writes an Illinois woman. "I believe that biblically the male is supposed to be the spiritual head of the household. But it's not that way in my marriage."

I received many letters from Christian wives/moms who feel frustrated and helpless in their inability to get their husbands to spiritually lead their families. Listen to some of their comments:

A North Carolina mother writes: "Few women in my church are married to Christian men who are willing to take the religious leadership role in the home. Women must perform that role along with hundreds of other roles. Unmarried women tell me it's difficult to even find a man whose father has been a role model in the area of religious leadership in the home."

"The number one problem today is what it has always been," claims a California mother. "Husbands won't fill the role of spiritual head of the home."

A New Mexico mother complains: "Men are not disciplined or taught, by parents or the church, how to be spiritual leaders in their homes."

"We women have to assume the spiritual head of the family because our husbands will not," explains an Oregon mom.

"Women don't want to take the leadership role for spiritual matters in the family," a Wisconsin mother writes. "But there are so many men in our families today who are either absent from the family, or do not go to church, and women are forced to take over spiritual roles. It's not really a 'want-to' situation, but a forced one."

"Some husbands are clueless about leading a family spiritually," writes an Alabama woman. "Leadership is sadly lacking in our homes."

A Missouri wife and mother acknowledges: "We need our husbands to be the spiritual leaders in our homes. Many of them did not grow up with a father who was a spiritual role model and do not truly understand this concept."

"More than anything else," states a California mom, "we need husbands who are able to step into the big shoes of being our spiritual head. With that in place, 99.9 percent of all other issues simply fade away."

I heard from many Christian wives and mothers who wish their pastors would challenge and train men to become the spiritual heads of their homes.

A mother of three writes: "I think pastors really need to help equip the men of the church to be godly fathers and husbands. Most women wish their husbands would be the spiritual leaders of the family. Many women are solely responsible for the spiritual focus and training in their homes."

Another writes: "Women are hurting because their husbands aren't being the spiritual leader in the home. That creates insecurity in women, and sometimes a sense of guilt, when their household isn't aligned according to God's Word. If pastors could lead the men to be the spiritual leaders in their homes, the fathers would be the best 'direct' pastor for their families."

"So many men are not heading spiritually the families in younger generations, and they need guidance from the church to do so. Younger women seem to be in charge of everything in the family," writes a Washington, D.C., mother.

"Many women are yearning for their husband to take their role as the family's spiritual leader, to seriously 'step up to the plate' and embrace this biblical command," says an Alabama woman. "I wish pastors would preach about the seriousness of this responsibility from the pulpit, and encourage men to take this burden off their wives. The reason a lot of women take over this role as spiritual leader is because if they don't, it won't get done. Many men abdicate this responsibility because they are married to strong-willed or controlling, confident women. But deep down even these women want their husbands to take on this role and release them from the burden. When men are truly serving in their God-given role as spiritual leader of their family, then women can step down, submit, and everything else falls into place—just as God has designed it."

An interesting note: Out of numerous survey responses stating this problem, only one woman blamed today's Christian wife for a husband's spiritual leadership failure. She writes: "I believe the number one problem church women face *is not allowing their husbands* to be the spiritual leader. So many women use the excuse that they just have strong personalities. Some like taking on that spiritual leadership."

What happens when women don't get help?

Listen to this Illinois mom: "When our men fail to grow spiritually, women lose heart and become defeated. I've even seen them leave the church. They just sit back with their apathetic husbands and lose the spiritual ground they once conquered."

"Lack of spiritual leadership by husbands in our homes causes a huge dilemma for women. We don't know whether or not to assume this role. If we do, we are called 'not submissive'; if we don't, then there is no spiritual leadership in the home for the children. What is a woman to do?" asks a Florida mom.

Why do some Christian husbands and fathers refuse to go to church?

David Murrow, in his book, *Why Men Hate Going to Church,* claims that many men think today's church is too "feminine." He writes that most men want a church where they are challenged by risk, change, conflict, variety, adventure, competition, daring, pleasure, independence, and expansion. On the other hand, he claims, most women want safety, stability, harmony, predictability, protection, comfort, nurture, support, and all those other "feminine" things women usually find in today's church.[15]

He asserts that most masculine men hate going to church because "men find the church too feminine for their liking." And Murrow asks: "So what? Can't men just get over all this macho stuff?" He answers: "No, they can't. You might as well ask a woman to get over her maternal instincts. The fact is, men's bodies, brains, histories, and cultures make it nearly impossible for them to flourish in today's church environment."[16]

Murrow makes an interesting point, but while most congregations do have more women than men in attendance and membership, I often see "masculine men" attending and heartily participating in today's churches.

These are just a few of the obstacles some women face in their mothering. Also consider the challenges of the mother who is suffering from physical illness or a debilitating handicap; dealing with mental health/emotional problems such as depression, anxiety, excess stress, past abortion guilt, etc.; married to a husband who has physical, mental, emotional, spiritual, and/ or addiction issues, battering problems, etc.; suffering from deep financial loss, bankruptcy, homelessness, etc.; trying to parent wayward children or children from a blended family; and/or taking full-time care of elderly or sick parents or in-laws.

A CHILD'S SPIRITUAL EDUCATION

Christian mothers today voice great concern over the spiritual education of their children. They believe God's Word when it tells them to "train a child in the way he should go, and when he is old he will not turn from it" (Proverbs 22:6). They want their children to know and to love God. "I want him to know the difference between 'knowing about God' and 'knowing God personally,'" writes one mother. They also want their offspring to do the future work God has planned for them—work that has eternal significance in God's plan. They try to teach their children to strive for the eternal things of life, not the quickly fading temporary things; to know the difference between those things that will last beyond them and those things that will not last beyond an hour, a year, or a lifetime. In addition, they want their children to build strong marriages as faithful and committed spouses, and to one day be responsible and loving parents who lead their own children to love God and serve him.

Christian mothers also want to know that their children's eternal souls will one day stand in Christ's presence for eternity. In these days of fragile families, high divorce rates, and dysfunctional homes, moms look to the pastor and church for help with the spiritual education of their children.

"Children should be taught about God in a simple, loving way," writes Joseph Girzone, "so they can learn to trust Him and begin to know Him as a kind and loving Father who made them, not perfectly but with all they need to grow in His love. They could be taught about Jesus and about His life and how He lived and how He loved people. They could be taught about Jesus as the Good Shepherd who cared for the hurting and the troubled sheep, so they can learn to run to Him when they have problems, and when they fall and make mistakes."[17]

Not long ago, I read a brief item in *Parade* magazine reporting a hiking magazine's misprint: "Britain's hiking magazine, *Trail*, apologized after its February issue contained a route that would lead climbers off the edge of the 4,409-foot peak on the north face of Ben Nevis, a Scottish mountain. The editor of *Trail* acknowledged that the magazine had inadvertently deleted the first of two crucial bearings that are needed to get off the summit if caught in bad weather."

Parade's editors added a humorous postscript: "If their readership declines, we'll know why."[18]

Christian mothers legitimately fear that if their children don't learn about "Jesus as the Good Shepherd," and if they don't get their Christian "bearings," they might end up on the wrong spiritual path and risk life and soul destruction.

Theologian Elizabeth Achtemeier writes: "Parents must pass on the language and knowledge of the biblical faith and the traditions of Christian belief and practice to their children, or their children will not be Christians but will fall victim to the hundreds of ideologies and spiritualities that are waiting to include them in their idolatrous folds."[19]

The church, as well as parents, must also pass on the language, knowledge, and traditions of Christian belief to the children.

HOW YOU CAN HELP CHRISTIAN MOMS

Christian mothers need encouragement from the church in order to raise their children to love Christ. They beg for Christian women—in "whatever role they can serve" (mother, grandmother, aunt, neighbor, church member, or teacher) to help them. A Florida mother writes: "We need to be challenged, but not distracted, from our most important mission. I see validating and encouraging mothers on child raising as a wide-open mission field."

Christian mothers need to be introduced to theologically sound family Bible studies they can do together at home. They yearn to be a family that together prays and studies God's Word.

Moms are asking for times of church activities that will bring mom, dad, and children together as a family rather than separate and send them to different parts of the church. They are begging for help with their fragile families in such areas as communication and problem solving.[20]

Today's moms want pastors to instill within their children's minds respect for parental authority. An Indiana mother writes: "Women want the pastor to help them by saying things to their kids like: 'Children, obey and respect your parents.'" Another complains: "We are tired of pastors who are trying to be popular with the kids by saying things the kids will like, when our entire society encourages kids to judge their parents and disrespect authority.... We need pastors to occasionally work into those sermons that children should obey and respect their parents. Even in non-Christian cultures around the world, parents and authority figures are still respected. But today, even in the church, this is not true."

Moms are asking for church-sponsored parenting classes to teach both mom and dad to be better parents and more astute Bible teachers to their children. Many women wanted pastors to encourage fathers to spend more time with their children. An Iowa mother writes: "We wish our husbands would be home more, and be more emotionally present—in actions and words, not just in body—to us and the children. What else is more important than a man's wife and kids?"

Christian mothers want to be taught how—in a practical, workable way—to incorporate Sunday's sermon (as well as other Bible teaching materials) into the entire week, in order to theologically train their children on a daily basis. "The Old Testament commands us not only to impress

God's words on our hearts and souls," writes Chuck Colson, "we're also told, 'Teach them to your children, talking about them when you sit at home and when you walk along the road, when you lie down and when you get up' (Deuteronomy 11:19). In modern lingo, that might include when you are taking them to soccer practice, watching a video, or sharing a pizza together."[21]

Moms ask that the pastor put more emphasis on children's and youth programs at church. A mom from Ohio writes: "I want my children to receive a strong Christian foundation at church. If a pastor doesn't make sure there are resources and training for the children and youth, the church will surely die."

Mothers want theologically qualified Sunday school and Bible study teachers for their children. They want Christian teachers who are well-versed in Scripture and serious about Bible study; who love children and love teaching children; who have God-given spiritual gifts that enable and equip them to work with children; and who are both male and female. (This is especially true for the child who has no male authority/father figure in his everyday life.) They also want their children taught by married couples within the church, who will take turns teaching Sunday school, and rotate the teaching responsibilities with other married couples in the church. They want Sunday school and nursery positions to be filled by church members other than the child's own parents.

WHAT CHRISTIAN PARENTS ASK THE CHURCH BODY TO DO

Christian mothers believe it takes a church to raise a child. "We all, as Christian parents and church members, have the heavy responsibility of being teachers and examples to our young people," a New Mexico mother writes. "The children are bombarded on every side with the world's godless thinking."

The pastor can lead the entire church body to help Christian parents raise godly children. The church can support families with daily prayers. They can love their children and, as a congregation, help guide them toward Christ. Congregants can seek to understand, tolerate, forgive, and accept their children's "childish behavior" in church and worship services. They can invite young children into the adult Sunday morning/evening worship services. (Many mothers feel that their children are often too quickly escorted out of the worship services and placed in child care during that important teaching time. They ask: "How will my children learn to function well in church if they don't have that worship opportunity at a young age?") The church body can make worship services and sermons more "child friendly" and welcoming to their children. Most parents want their children to feel comfortable in the church, to look forward to worship and church activities, and to enjoy learning about God.

"It is very important for young women and mothers to know that their children are being cared for, being taught the Word of God creatively, and are happy while at church," a Mississippi mother writes.

CHILDREN "DRIVE" A WOMAN'S SCHEDULE

Christian mothers want their pastors to know that a mother's children often set her time and energy priorities. "For the Christian mother, her children drive everything: schedules, time commitments, even satisfaction with church programs and services," writes a Tennessee mother. "Pastors should always 'think children' when they consider their ministry to the women of their churches." They also want pastors to know that today's Christian mothers are exhausted trying to raise godly children, work full- or part-time jobs outside and inside the home, take care of husbands, aging parents, in-laws, and so on.

Children demand a woman's role be that of a "mother," but women are much more than one role. "Roles are necessary because they give structure to our lives ... roles tell us what we may expect people to do, but they do not tell us who those people *are*.... Women receive a cultural message that being a mother is the center of their identity. Motherhood is a role, not an identity." Motherhood is "not the entirety of a woman's life, nor is it the mark of her identity as a woman." A woman's true identity is in Christ.[22]

Pastors greatly help mothers today when they create church-sponsored times of support and fellowship so moms can get together with other mothers to learn from each other, pray for each other and their families, and support and encourage each other in the difficult job of child rearing. Most women need close friends. In fact, studies show that women who have one or two close reciprocal friendships have stronger marriages than women who expect their husbands to be all things to them.[23]

Even the most loving and dedicated mom needs an occasional church-sponsored (and church-encouraged) retreat away from her children. She may also need some practical, hands-on help! "Our children are driving us crazy," writes an Ohio mom. "No one helps each other anymore, it seems, and those of us who live away from family don't get many 'breaks' from the little ones."

Even though today's mothers love and care for their children, some find the job of motherhood to be difficult, confusing, and often lacking joy. Mothers are often "compromised by messages that parenting should be a source of ongoing fulfillment. The reality is that parenting can be boring, frustrating, anxiety provoking, and infuriating.... Messages that mothering should be a source of endless fulfillment create guilt, anxiety, and shame for women who don't feel particularly thrilled by their role."[24]

PASTORS AND MOMS – THE JOBS ARE SIMILAR

If anyone should understand both a pastor's role and a mother's role, it is the pastor and the mother! They have much in common. Both pastor and mom have the responsibility to spiritually shape the minds and hearts of others. Both are "on call" twenty-four hours a day for emergencies, crises, or just "the need to talk." They are responsible to God for the doctrine they preach and teach. Both know fully the eternal soul consequences when someone they know/love rejects Christ. Both pastor and mom know their work is never done.

They each carry the emotional burdens of those who hurt. They serve as full-time nurturers, encouragers, and pray-ers. They both know they can't "please all the people all the time." No matter how much each loves and gives, both will receive his and her share of unfair criticism. They know their time, energy, and life-work revolves around God and others. Both often feel great frustration, guilt, and anxiety about their roles.

Is it any wonder that the Good Shepherd himself uses the metaphor of a shepherd and his sheep (a pastor and his congregation) to describe God's parental love and nurture for those in his charge (John 10:1–18), or that Jesus employs the "hen and her chicks" image (a mother and her children) to describe his concern and heartbreak over those he loves and wants to protect (Luke 13:34)?

Today's Christian woman wants her pastor to know that:

- Her children's relationship to Christ is her primary concern and goal.
- Often she is solely responsible for her child's physical, emotional, mental, financial, and spiritual health.
- Motherhood is a difficult and exhausting role, and she can feel frustrated and guilty.
- As a mother, she often faces situational obstacles, and she needs your special understanding and help.
- She may be married to an unbeliever who discourages her (and her children's) church involvement.
- She may be married to a Christian who refuses to spiritually lead the family.
- She often is the spiritual head of her family—not because she wants to be, but because she has to be.
- She hopes you will challenge and train men in the church to become the spiritual heads of their homes.
- She is very concerned about her child's spiritual education, and needs the church's help.

PART 4

WOMEN'S
PERCEPTIONS
OF PASTORS

CHAPTER 8

"PASTOR, WHEN YOU PREACH ..."

A preacher can do only three things with an idea: explain it, prove it, and apply it ... [in other words:] What does the text mean? Is it true? And so what?[1]

Alice P. Mathews

MANY CHRISTIAN WOMEN TODAY view the sermon—the proclamation of the gospel—as the centerpiece of the worship experience. They yearn for the serious pastor to stand with integrity in the pulpit, open his Bible to a particular text, and preach deep, accurate, biblical theology. They want him to explain the text and tell them what it means; prove the text and show them its truth; and tell them how to apply the text to their everyday lives. They desperately need God's truth in his Word to get through the difficult and demanding week ahead. They depend on it!

WOMEN WANT PREACHING TO BE BIBLE BASED

Most survey responses asked that more Scripture be taught in sermons. Many women told me they had recently left churches due to the lack of scriptural teaching in sermons.

A new Barna study shows that "a *faith revolution* is redefining 'church.'" He writes: "There is a much larger segment of Americans who are currently leaving churches precisely because they want more of God in their life but cannot get what they need from a local church. They have decided to get serious about their faith by piecing together a more robust faith experience.

Instead of going to church, they have chosen to be the church, in a way that harkens back to the church detailed in the book of Acts."[2]

More than anything else, women want their pastors to "preach the Word" (2 Timothy 4:2).

"The one thing that has encouraged me, and equipped me most to serve my family and others, is the Word—verse by verse study of the Holy Scriptures," writes an Alabama woman.

"Please, Pastor," writes another, "preach the Word clearly and deeply."

"Focus on Scripture!" writes a Minnesota mom.

"Teach the Bible," writes another, "and allow the Holy Spirit to convict your congregation."

"I need a clear interpretation of Scripture," explains an Ohio woman. "I wish pastors knew that women fight against the subtle pressures of culture as much as men. They need to have clear definitions from Scripture so they can *biblically* influence culture—and not the other way around."

"We need to be fed the Word of God," writes a Virginia woman, "We need spiritual food to face the pressures and temptations of life."

Another writes: "Women today face the problem of not being familiar enough with God's Word."

"I want to know God more intimately and to know his Word more deeply. I want to hear more depth during Sunday services," says a Florida woman.

Another begs: "Please, Pastor, preach the gospel of Jesus Christ as it is written."

An Illinois woman writes: "I am grateful that my pastor understands that women and men alike have the exact same problem: their own sin—and they need the exact same solution: the gospel. The best thing my pastor can do for me, as a young woman in his congregation, is 'preach the Word, in season and out of season.' If he does this faithfully, then all women will be empowered through the Word and by the Spirit.... When any pastor rightly divides the Word of truth, Christian women will know that God is able to make all grace abound to them."

OUR NATION – A SMORGASBORD OF RELIGIOUS BELIEFS!

According to the Barna study, we are a nation where "nine out of ten adults own at least one Bible," and "eight out of ten consider themselves to be Christian," but you'd never know it from the "smorgasbord of religious beliefs professed by most people!" Many people today have adopted beliefs that "conflict with the teachings of the Bible and their church."

Did you know that 44 percent of adults believe that "the Bible, the Koran and the Book of Mormon are all different expressions of the same spiritual truths"? And that only 38 percent of Americans reject that idea?

What do a majority of Americans (54 percent) believe about truth? They think "truth can be discovered only through logic, human reasoning, and personal experience."

"Over the past twenty years we have seen the nation's theological views slowly become less aligned with the Bible. Americans still revere the Bible and like to think of themselves as Bible-believing people, but the evidence suggests otherwise. Christians have increasingly been adopting spiritual views that come from Islam, Wicca, secular humanism, the Eastern religions, and other sources. Because we remain a largely Bible-illiterate society, few are alarmed or even aware of the slide toward syncretism — a belief system that blindly combines beliefs from many different faith perspectives."[3]

It is imperative that pastors today focus worship services on Scripture. Thom Rainer writes: "The clear teachings of biblical truth are demanding and convicting. The Holy Spirit speaks through God's Word in such a way that the cost of discipleship is understood. No higher expectations could be placed upon believers than these truths of Scripture."[4]

Philip Yancey writes: "I find it remarkable that this ... diverse collection of manuscripts written over a period of a millennium by several dozen authors, possesses as much unity as it does. To appreciate this feat, imagine a book begun five hundred years before Columbus and just now completed. The Bible's striking unity is one strong sign that God directed its composition. By using a variety of authors and cultural situations, God developed a complete record of what he wants us to know; amazingly, the parts fit together in such a way that a single story does emerge."[5]

Christian women want their pastors to teach them this Word. They also have a number of other suggestions concerning the pastor's worship service.

1. Carefully and Prayerfully Prepare the Sermon

Women ask that pastors pray and study and allow themselves to be guided by the Holy Spirit as they prepare their worship service sermons.

"I need for my pastor to study and prepare sermons that will help my growth as a Christian," explains a Tennessee woman. "I need more scriptural 'meat.'"

"Preach the Bible — study hard — don't pull sermons off the Internet," advises another.

"Know that I love you and support you, and I appreciate the time you spend in study and prayer before God," writes a Alabama woman. "It shows in your messages and I really desire the spiritual food you provide each week."

2. Get Rid of "Entertainment" in the Worship Services

Most women go to church to worship God and to hear his Holy Word preached. They are tired of Sunday morning "entertainment" in the service. They want worship, not performance. The world offers them entertainment without ceasing. They expect and want something different from church.

According to pastor/church growth consultant Richard Krejcir: "Some preachers strive to make the gospel more appealing by watering down its message.... A healthy church will never sacrifice the integrity of the Bible or neuter its message."

Krejcir advises Christians who are looking for a church community to "first look for a place where truth is preached from the Bible—where God's Word is seen as living, relevant, changeless, and inerrant, rather than just a 'good book' filled with advice on how to be a more loving, moral person."[6]

A Michigan woman writes: "I would like more teaching from Scripture and less entertainment in church worship. I'm weary of all the skits and sing-a-longs and interpretive dance. Many of us don't have a strong enough foundation in God's Word to face life's struggles. Preachers need to help build strong Christians so that we can weather the storms in life. Many times I feel we lose sight of the real reason we attend church."

Another complains: "The worship service seems to be all fluff these days."

I love author Annie Dillard's comments as she describes the potential power of the Holy Spirit in our worship services, and how unaware Christians are of his power:

"On the whole," Dillard writes, "I do not find Christians, outside of the catacombs, sufficiently sensible of conditions. Does anyone have the foggiest idea what sort of power we so blithely invoke? Or, as I suspect, does no one believe a word of it?"

Dillard compares today's church to "children playing on the floor with their chemistry sets, mixing up a batch of TNT to kill a Sunday morning. It is madness to wear ladies' straw hats to church; we should all be wearing crash helmets. Ushers should issue life preservers and signal flares.... For the sleeping God may someday wake and take offense, or the waking God may draw us out to where we can never return."[7]

Crash helmets? Life preservers? Flares? What would happen if Christians today *did* invoke the power of the Holy Spirit? How lightly we can take the worship of God even when Jesus took it so seriously! Women tell me that some churches today differ very little from the community's country clubs.

3. Show Women How to Apply God's Word to Their Lives

Women need for pastors to show them how to apply God's Word to their everyday lives, especially those who face challenges and difficulties.

A woman from Mississippi writes: "I think it is important for pastors to help us apply the Bible more to our daily life, and show us how to claim the joy that Christ gives."

Another responds: "I want the worship service to engage both my heart and my head so that I may love God with all my heart, strength, soul, and mind—during everyday life."

A woman from Ohio says: "I want my pastor to know that I appreciate very much the teaching of God's truths, and I'd like more practical applications given. He often tells me *what* I should do, now please tell me *how* to do it!"

In her book *Preaching That Speaks to Women*, Alice Mathews writes: "A fundamental aim of preaching is to empower listeners to incorporate what they have heard from Scripture into solutions to the challenges of everyday life."[8]

I also discovered that many women want their pastor to enable them, through God's Word, to reach out to other women around them. One Midwestern woman writes: "I would like to see pastors taking the lead in guiding the women of their congregations to not be satisfied with spiritual status quo, but to be keenly interested in how a relationship with Christ calls women to look beyond themselves into a world of need."

4. Offer Compassion and Special Instruction to the Hurting Women

A Texas woman writes: "We all have emotional needs—our hearts are broken over something or someone. Please, Pastor, consider that in preparing your sermon. Be sure the Greek translation doesn't upstage the broken hearts. Allow the Holy Spirit to confirm and bestow the compassion that's needed."

"Women on every pew in the church are hurting for one reason or another on any given Sunday," writes another. "When preachers handle God's Word effectively, the Holy Spirit will speak to each open heart with healing and conviction."

"Preach sermons that speak to hurting women—divorced, widowed, infertile women, etc.," suggests a New England woman.

A woman experiencing serious marital problems writes: "First of all, I know and believe in the power of the Word of God ... however, I personally wish my pastor knew how to address issues that are at the heart of women like me ... women who are divorced or separated, women who are seeking guidance and direction for their lives, women who desire to know and learn how to touch the heart of God and to enter into his presence, women who strive for righteousness but still fall short of God's glory. I wish my pastor incorporated into his sermons those things that speak to my needs."

"The biggest problem church women face today is an improper view of God," says a California woman. "We have been wounded in our pasts (many of us), and we view God the way we see men, our fathers, husbands, etc. We don't realize and understand God's infinite love for us."

A New Mexico woman praises her pastor: "I am blessed with a pastor who does a very commendable job of communicating both biblical truth and true compassion to the women of our congregation."

5. Stop Stereotyping Single Women in the Congregation

More than one single woman wants her pastor to preach sermons that don't always stereotype the single adults in the congregation.

"My pastor just assumes that every single woman in his church is desperate to get married!" writes a young single woman. "It always comes through in his sermons!"

From Alabama: "As a single woman, I wish pastors would learn how to preach more messages that speak to the hearts and needs of singles. I am burned out on topics like, 'Being Single and Satisfied,' 'Lonely But Not Alone,' and 'How to Choose the Right Mate.' I wish pastors would spend time talking with us who are single to find out what our needs are. We are such a diverse group—some of us have never been married, some have been divorced, some have children, some are in their twenties or thirties or forties or fifties. We are all unique. We each have different goals in life."

6. Use More Stories and Examples from the Lives of Biblical Women

Women constantly hear pastors preach on the triumphant men in the Bible. They want to hear more about the Bible's triumphant women.

A Wisconsin woman writes: "I would like my pastor to know my desire to hear sermons/teachings from the pulpit that include godly women from the Bible, like Deborah for example. Men have something to learn from the Bible's godly women, just as we have much to learn from Paul and other men. I don't understand why preaching about women (other than Mary, Jesus' mother, at Christmastime) is reserved only for women's Bible studies or Sunday school classes."

A woman from South Carolina writes: "I wish our pastor wouldn't use so many male-oriented and sports illustrations to make his preaching points. Some women can't relate to them much at all." But another wants her pastor to know that "just because we might not understand sports examples doesn't mean we cannot understand spiritual/doctrinal issues."

Says another: "I would like for any pastor to understand that no matter what he *says* in his sermons ... what he *is* comes through louder and clearer."

THE THREE BIG "PREACHING MISTAKES"

While some pastors may think these following three issues are trivial, be assured that they are not trivial to the women in your church. Women, in unison and in all seriousness, tell me pastors must—at all costs—avoid making these three major mistakes when they preach to women:

Do Not Make Jokes about Women That Are Insulting, Demeaning, or Rudely Stereotypical

A popular, highly admired evangelical preacher stood in the pulpit and asked: "Do you know the difference between an angry woman and a Doberman pinscher?" (The answer): "Lipstick." Sixty percent of the congregation did not laugh. Nor did they hear anything else he said after that crude joke. A Kentucky woman writes: "Women want respect from the pulpit—no jokes about women, or degrading comments toward women."

Don't Ever Mention or Refer to a Woman's Age

Like it or not, many women are self-conscious about their age—especially after they have celebrated their twenty-fifth birthday! They cringe on Mother's Day when the roses-laden pastor inevitably asks from the pulpit: "Will our oldest mother stand up?" And pastors wonder why no one stands! On Mother's Day at one Southern Baptist church, a pastor thought he was honoring elderly Mrs. Jones, when he asked: "Mrs. Jones, you are the oldest mother in the congregation. Will you please lead us in our closing prayer?" Mrs. Jones slowly stood up, white-knuckled the pew in front of her, and said loudly: "No, I won't!"

Always View Women as Unique and Individual

Today's Christian women have much in common, but they are also individuals. That's why, when Lazarus died, Jesus comforted Martha and her sister Mary in different ways. Martha needed a theological dissertation about the resurrection, so Jesus preached to her on an academic level. Mary, on the other hand, needed someone simply to cry with her. So Jesus wept. (See John 11.)

Just as all men don't like fly fishing or baseball or aren't all mechanically inclined, women aren't the same either. For example, while some women love to cook, other women hate to cook. Some women like to shop; other women hate to shop. Some single women want to get married; other single women want to stay single. Some women want to become mothers; other women don't want children. You get the idea.

Today's Christian woman wants her pastor to know that:

- She wants and craves deep theology and God's Word preached from the pulpit.
- She expects her pastor to study God's Word, be guided by the Holy Spirit, and prayerfully prepare his sermons.
- She is weary of human-centered entertainment that replaces biblical preaching.
- She needs for her pastor to show her how to apply God's Word to her everyday life.
- Hurting women sit in pews all around her, and they need compassionate and scriptural teaching through sermons.
- She resents female stereotyping in any form. Stereotyping wrongly categorizes her and hurts her. She is unique and individual in her person, desires, and goals.
- She would appreciate it if he would use more female biblical characters and female-oriented illustrations in his sermons.
- She expects her pastor to show respect for her, and for all the church's women, from his pulpit.
- She resents jokes and comments about women that are insulting, demeaning, or in poor taste.

Recommendation

A resource for pastors that I highly recommend is Dr. Alice P. Mathews' book, *Preaching That Speaks to Women* (Baker Academic, 2003). Dr. Mathews is the Lois W. Bennett Distinguished Associate Professor of Educational Ministries and Women's Ministries at Gordon-Conwell Theological Seminary in Wenham, Massachusetts.

"PASTOR, PLEASE ALLOW ME TO MINISTER TO YOU AND YOUR FAMILY"

> *Most pastors work long hours, are constantly on-call, often sacrifice time with family to tend to congregational crises, carry long-term debt from the cost of seminary, and receive below-average compensation in return for performing a difficult job. Trained in theology, they are expected to master leadership, politics, finance, management, psychology and conflict resolution. Pastoring must be a calling from God if one is to garner a sense of satisfaction and maintain unflagging commitment to that job.*[1]
>
> **George Barna**

THE PASTOR TODAY has an almost impossible job!

"I believe it's harder today to be a pastor than any other period in history," writes a North Carolina woman. "The church has too many expectations of him. Congregations today are made up of people from a variety of backgrounds, and each holds such unrealistic expectations. My heart breaks for today's pastors. I have seen countless dedicated and courageous men deeply hurt by unfair, constant criticism. Their wives are hurt as well."

Many church members often expect their pastor to be accountable to God, his own family, and his church family for his every word and action; be constantly "on call" and available to anyone who needs him at a moment's notice; and personally shoulder the emotional and spiritual burdens of his family and congregation. He is expected be an expert in every field of leadership, administration, and pastoral care; accept criticism and confrontation with a smile; know how to settle all disputes and conflicts within the church and community; and deal with congregational "troublemakers" who purposely disrupt fellowship and cause rift. He must also minister equally to members both kind and rude, complimentary and critical, supportive and unsupportive.

And that's not all. Church members also often expect him to preach effectively to every person in every pew, notwithstanding the fact that his church members—children and adults—typically range in age from birth to ninety-plus, are male and female, rich and poor, educated and uneducated, employed and unemployed, sick and well, of sound or unsound mind, theologically literate or theologically illiterate, devoted to God or spiritually lukewarm. They expect him to guide members to spiritual maturity regardless of the fact that many congregants show no desire to mature as Christians; rarely read the Bible or pray; lack any commitment to loving and serving God or people; are involved in no personal ministries to church or community; see little relevance in teaching scriptural principles to their offspring; and take scarce interest in God, others, worship attendance, church participation, and monetary giving.

These superhuman expectations often extend to the pastor's wife (and children). The pastor and his wife are to live in a "glass house," and often an "open house," allowing church members unlimited access not only into their home but into their personal family life, issues, and struggles. They're expected to maintain a perfect, conflict-free marriage that serves as an example for all the engaged and married couples in the church, and to be devoted, exemplary parents—June and Ward Cleavers who teach church families how to successfully raise their own children. And, of course, they're expected to work hard together *in* the church and *for* the church—on one small paycheck; attend and participate in all church-related and church-sponsored events and activities; and basically just be "all things to all people" in the church and community.

But thankfully that's not the whole story.

THE WOMEN OF YOUR CHURCH STAND BEHIND YOU

The survey responses show that most Christian women in churches today—especially those with children—understand well the pressures, demands, unrealistic expectations, and constant interruptions a church pastor faces. They also know that pastors often receive unfair criticism, as

well as limited gratitude, from church members. That's why they want you
to know a few things, including:

They Love, Appreciate, and Support You, and Pray for You and Your Family

"I want my pastor to know how much we love him and his family, and how
we constantly support them with prayer," an Alabama woman writes.

"I want to thank my pastor and his wife for all the work they do in the
church," writes another. "I will be praying more for them in the future."

Another writes: "My pastor's dedication to God speaks loudly to me!
I appreciate his love and passion for the Lord. It rubs off on the whole
congregation!"

"I appreciate my pastor's encouragement," says another. "I know I will
make it when I hear him say: 'You are going to make it. Christ lives within
you.'"

They Want to Encourage You in Your Personal Prayer Life and Spiritual Growth

Some recent studies show that today's church pastor often lacks personal
prayer time. "Though prayer is the communication vehicle through which
a relationship with God develops," writes Terry C. Muck, "many pastors
struggle to maintain a consistent prayer life."[2]

When pastors deal with a deficient prayer life and an irregular and
inadequate quiet time with God, it can quickly sap the power of their
ministry. A recent study by Ellison Research shows that "only 16 percent
of Protestant ministers across the country are very satisfied with their personal prayer life. Another 47 percent are somewhat satisfied with it. Thirty
percent are somewhat dissatisfied, and 7 percent are very dissatisfied with
their prayer life."[3]

The study also reveals that today's pastors most commonly pray about
these six things: the needs of individual members of their congregations;
the congregation's spiritual health; spiritual growth for their church; wisdom in leading their church; the right things to say in a sermon; and their
own personal spiritual growth.[4]

"My pastor 'walks the walk' and 'talks the talk,'" writes a woman from
California. "It thrills my soul when he speaks of what God is doing in his
life—his own spiritual journey. I want him to share with us his struggles
and heartbreaks, and to tell us how he is facing adversity."

An Illinois woman writes: "Pastor, we don't expect you to be spiritually perfect. You are allowed to make mistakes, need prayers, and have human feelings of anger, fear, sadness, etc."

They Are Concerned about Your Family Life

The vast majority of Protestant clergy believe "there is additional pressure on pastors' families," that "churchgoers often expect pastors' families to be 'better than' other people's families." A majority also worry that a pastor's role leaves him "with insufficient time" for his own family.[5]

The good news is that pastors today feel confident that, in the event of a personal family crisis, they would receive the necessary support from their church members. "Sixty-one percent are strongly confident of getting the support they need, with another 33 percent somewhat confident of this; only 6 percent express little or no confidence their church will support them."[6]

And what is the state of today's pastoral families? Thankfully, only about "5 percent of pastors report a very unhealthy relationship with their spouse." While that seems a small number, it also "means there are over ten thousand individual pastors with serious marital problems right now," and that doesn't include the marital problems of "associate ministers or other staff in Protestant churches, nor of those who have left the ministry because of these issues."[7]

"I'm grateful my pastor has a wife he loves, and they are both committed to Christ," writes a West Virginia woman.

From Washington, D.C.: "My pastor and wife communicate well with each other. She keeps him informed about what the women in the church need."

From Oklahoma: "My pastor is a very good example of what a Christian husband and father should be. He sets an excellent example for us."

They Want to Minister to You and Your Family

Women in the church realize that all people—*even* pastors (and maybe *especially* pastors)—need concerned and caring ministry from other Christians.

A North Carolina woman writes: "All my thoughts toward ministers basically revolve around great admiration, respect, and empathy. I long for ways to minister to them more."

An Alabama woman confesses: "Women would like for their pastors to know that they grieve when their pastor is hurting, yet are often not able to express their understanding adequately."

Some pastors think that receiving ministry from others represents a spiritual weakness. But Jesus' own example proves otherwise. Consider the times Jesus himself sought, allowed, accepted, or received specific ministry from others:

- Alone in the wilderness, after three grueling satanic temptations, Jesus accepted with gratitude the angels who came and "attended him" (Matthew 4:11).
- Jesus asked a group of men to follow him and help him in his ministry (Mark 1:14–20; 2:13–14; 3:13–19; Luke 5:1–11), and he accepted financial support and help from the women who traveled with him and his disciples during his ministry years (Mark 15:40–41).
- While at dinner in the home of a Pharisee in Nain, Jesus allowed a "sinful woman" to wash his dirty feet with her tears, dry them with her hair, and anoint him with expensive perfume (Luke 7:36–50).
- Jesus accepted two days of hospitality from the Samaritans when he visited their town (John 4:40).
- When he and his "congregation" were hungry, Jesus gratefully accepted five small barley loaves and two small fish from a boy (John 6:1–9).
- En route to Jerusalem, knowing he would face an angry crowd, Jesus stopped by the home of Mary and Martha in Bethany. He needed some loving encouragement (Luke 10:38–42).
- On the Mount of Olives, shortly before Jesus' arrest, he asked his disciples to pray with him. Sadly, they failed Jesus, and instead of praying, they slept (Luke 22:39–46).
- Jesus allowed Simon from Cyrene to help him carry his cross as he journeyed toward his crucifixion (Mark 15:21).
- When, from the cross, Jesus cried: "I am thirsty," he accepted and received the offered sponge soaked with wine vinegar (John 19:28–30).

Referring to Jesus' friendship with Mary and Martha, Brennan Manning writes, "Exhausted from the hurly-burly of ministry, heavyhearted with the intrigue of the Pharisees and the pettiness of the apostles, longing for female companionship, he seeks out his two dear friends." But when Martha seems more interested in preparing his supper and criticizing her sister, Mary, for not helping, Jesus responds: "'Cool it, Martha. We'll have the trout almondine later. I'm worn out, lonely, empty, and frightened. I'm heading to the Holy City, and as you know, a prophet must die in Jerusalem. Drop the frying pan, come over here, sit beside your sister, and hold my hand. I need you. Mary's got a grip on where I'm at. She knows that I'm fully human, have a sensitive human heart, and long to be treated as a man who is human.'"[8]

When a pastor and his family accept and receive the love, concern, prayers, and practical help from women in the church, two things happen: The pastor and his family receive ministry and, at the same time, they give women in the church the opportunity to minister to someone they love—their pastor and his family. Everyone benefits.

Again and again in the surveys, women express their desire to minister to the pastor and his family as they work together in the difficult task of church ministry. In the next chapter, we'll see how women in the church want their pastors to minister to them.

SURVEY SUMMARY

Today's Christian woman wants her pastor to know that:

- She wants to personally minister to him and his family, and wants him to tell her how best to do that.
- She understands the pressures and demands of today's church pastor and his family.
- She loves, appreciates, and supports him, and prays for him and his family.
- She wants to encourage him in his personal prayer life and spiritual growth.
- She hopes he will give her the opportunity to minister to him and his family and, using Jesus as his example, will accept and receive her ministry.

CHAPTER

10

"PASTOR, PLEASE MINISTER TO ME AND MY FAMILY"

Jesus treated women with respect, dignity, importance, forgiveness, hope, affirmation, praise, love, honor, kindness, compassion, tenderness, understanding, care, and concern. He gives today's pastors excellent examples to follow as they interact with, relate, and minister to, the women in their church.

PASTOR, HAVE YOU EVER read through the Gospels just to see how Jesus specifically related and ministered to women? It's quite an eye-opening study, especially when you also consider how Jesus treated women differently than he treated men.

Let's spend the next few pages doing an abbreviated New Testament survey of this very topic, after which we'll apply our insights to the needs of women in today's church.

HOW DID JESUS RELATE AND MINISTER TO WOMEN?

Jesus treated the women in his life and ministry with respect and dignity. He regarded women, and their eternal souls, as important to the kingdom of God. Consider some of Jesus' encounters with women:

Jesus and the Woman at Jacob's Well (John 4:1 – 42)

To witness to a specific woman at Jacob's well, Jesus traveled to Samaria, a town Jewish men purposely avoided. He approached the five-time-divorced woman with respect, even though Samaria's townsfolk treated her with hostility and disgust. Even the disciples questioned Jesus' dignified and unprecedented actions toward her: They "were surprised to find him talking with a woman" (v. 27). With respect for her mental ability to understand deep theological matters, Jesus presented her with the truth of the gospel (vv. 21 – 26) — a theology even his own disciples were sometimes slow to grasp. She understood it immediately, and she eagerly led many of her fellow townspeople to come to Christ (v. 39).

Women in the church today also want to be treated with respect and dignity. They want their pastors to realize the importance of a woman's soul, as well as the necessity of her ministry to the church.

Jesus and the Adulterous Woman (John 8:1 – 11)

As Jesus taught in the temple courts, some teachers and Pharisees brought an adulterous woman to him. To test him, they said: "Teacher, this woman was caught in the act of adultery. In the Law Moses commanded us to stone such women. Now what do you say?" (vv. 4 – 5). Jesus didn't condemn her, but offered her forgiveness and hope — the opportunity to start a new life void of sin (vv. 6 – 11).

Women in the church today yearn for forgiveness and a second chance at life. Pastors must offer them forgiveness for their offenses, thus demonstrating that God also forgives them and gives new opportunities to follow him.

Jesus and the Perfume-Anointing Woman (Luke 7:36 – 50)

When a woman interrupted the dinner party where Jesus was a guest, the Pharisees criticized and demeaned her anointment of Jesus' feet. Simon, the dinner host, insulted both Jesus and the woman: "If this man [Jesus] were a prophet, he would know who is touching him and what kind of woman she is — that she is a sinner" (v. 39).

But Jesus accepted her perfumed anointment, affirmed her in her faith, and praised her actions. "Therefore I tell you," Jesus told the fault-finding men, "her many sins have been forgiven — for she loved much" (v. 47).

Women today also need affirmation from their pastors. And when they do a job well, they crave the pastor's sincere praise.

Jesus and the Crippled Woman (Luke 13:10 – 17)

As previously noted in chapter five, when Jesus reached out with love and healed a crippled woman in the synagogue, he immediately became the target of the synagogue ruler's wrath. Jesus not only lovingly defended the woman, and her right to be healed, but he also honored her. "Should not this woman, *a daughter of Abraham*, whom Satan has kept bound for eighteen long years, be set free on the Sabbath day from what bound her?" Jesus asked (v. 16, my emphasis).

Women today yearn to be wholesomely loved and genuinely honored. A pastor's caring words can make a tremendous difference in a woman's life, and make her feel loved, treasured, and honored.

Jesus and the Grieving Widow (Luke 7:11 – 17) and Jesus and His Mother, Mary (John 19:25 – 27)

As Jesus traveled through Nain, he came upon a funeral in progress. A widow was burying her only son, her sole support. According to Luke, "When the Lord saw her, his heart went out to her and he said, 'Don't cry'" (v. 13). Then Jesus raised the grieving mother's son to life and gave him back to her.

Near the end of Jesus' earthly ministry, while suffering upon the cross, he with selfless concern made arrangements for his mother's future care. "Dear woman," Jesus said to Mary, "here is your son." And to John, Jesus said, "Here is your mother." John tells us "from that time on, this disciple took her into his home" (vv. 26 – 27).

Kindness and compassion are sorely lacking in our society today. We live in a fast-paced world overwhelmed by high-tech rudeness. The kind and compassionate pastor, through his Christlike actions, will speak volumes to a woman accustomed to rudeness and indifference.

Jesus and the Bleeding Woman (Luke 8:40 – 48)

Without Jesus' permission, a bleeding woman, who had suffered her incurable illness for a dozen years, reached out from the crowd and touched Jesus' cloak. His power immediately stopped her bleeding and restored her health. When Jesus confronted her, she fell at his feet and confessed her "crime." She expected his harsh rebuke. Instead Jesus responded to her with tenderness and understanding. "Daughter," he told her, "your faith has healed you. Go in peace" (v. 48).

Consider also Jesus' gentle physical touch when it came to women and/or their children. He touched the hand of Peter's fever-wracked mother-in-law and healed her (Matthew 8:15); he put his hands on the crippled woman in synagogue and made her well (Luke 13:13); he reached out and took the hand of Jairus's daughter and delivered her from death (8:43); he took babies and children in his arms to bless them (18:15; Mark 10:16).

Christian women today can travel through life never knowing tenderness and understanding from the men in their lives. The pastor who reaches out to hurting women in appropriate ways can teach them much about God's love, tenderness, acceptance, and understanding.

Note: The only example I can find of Jesus reacting to a woman's request with what might be considered rudeness or unkindness is when a Canaanite woman begged him to heal her demon-possessed daughter (see Matthew 15:21–28). At first Jesus offered her no response at all, yet she continued to cry out to him. Finally, he turned to her and said: "I was sent only to the lost sheep of Israel" (v. 24). What seemed an attitude of indifference toward her proved to be a test of her faith. And she passed the test! Matthew tells us that Jesus granted the woman's request and "her daughter was healed from that very hour" (v. 28).

HOW JESUS RELATED TO MEN

How did Jesus relate to the men around him? In many cases, he treated men like he treated women—with respect, dignity, forgiveness, hope, and affirmation (see, for example, Matthew 8:3; 20:34; Mark 7:33; 9:17–27; Luke 22:50–51; John 9:6–7; 13:4–5). Interestingly enough, however, most often Jesus did not respond as gently with men as he did with women. Jesus had a unique knowledge and understanding into the God-created natures of women, and how they drastically differ from those of men. And he repeatedly demonstrated that understanding and knowledge as he interacted with them.

With men, Jesus got right to the heart of the issue. He didn't mince words. He made his point quickly and effectively. For example:

Jesus Taught Men with Directness and Unquestioning Authority

No man had to ask Jesus what he meant when he spoke. Consider these statements (or my paraphrases thereof) in his Sermon on the Mount, likely preached to a crowd of mostly men: "Do not murder" (Matthew 5:21); "Do not commit adultery" (5:27); "Do not divorce your wife" (see 5:31–32); "Do not break your oath" (5:33); "Do not resist an evil person" (5:39); "Love your enemies" (5:44); "Do not announce your gifts to the needy" (see 6:1–2); "Do not be hypocrites when you pray" (see 6:5); "Forgive men when they sin against you" (6:14–15); "Fast in private" (see 6:16–18); "Do not store up treasure on earth" (see 6:19); "Do not judge others" (see 7:1–2). It's no wonder that "when Jesus had finished saying these things, the crowds were amazed at his teaching because he taught as one who had authority, and not as their teachers of the law" (7:28–29).

Jesus Often Harshly Disciplined His Male Disciples

When Galilee's storms threatened to destroy the disciples in their boat, and they cried out in unison, "Lord, save us! We're going to drown!" Jesus rebuked them. "You of little faith," he said, "why are you so afraid?" (See Matthew 8:23–27.)

When Peter tried to walk on the water with Jesus, and sank with doubt, Jesus lamented: "You of little faith, why did you doubt?" (14:31). When Peter asked Jesus to explain a parable, Jesus asked: "Are you still so dull?" (15:16). Another time Jesus rebuked the disciples: "You of little faith ... do you still not understand?" (16:8–9). Perhaps the greatest rebuke came when Jesus turned to Peter and shouted: "Get behind me, Satan! You are a stumbling block to me; you do not have in mind the things of God, but the things of men" (16:23).

Jesus Corrected Pharisees and Religious Leaders with Harsh Rebuke

Jesus regularly rebuked the Pharisees. When they reprimanded him for his Sabbath habits, he countered, "Haven't you read what David did?... Haven't you read in the Law?... If any of you has a sheep and it falls into a pit on the Sabbath, will you not take hold of it and lift it out?" (See Matthew 12:1–8, 11). When the Pharisees and teachers of the law asked Jesus for a miraculous sign, he called them "a wicked and adulterous generation" (12:38–39). On one occasion, Jesus denounced their failure to heed John the Baptist's message by saying, "The tax collectors and the prostitutes are entering the kingdom of God ahead of you" (21:31). On another, Jesus told them: "You belong to your father, the devil" (John 8:44). Again and again he called the Pharisees hypocrites (Matthew 23:13, 15, 23, 25, 27, 29); blind guides (23:16), white-washed tombs (23:27–28), snakes and vipers (23:33).

The most dramatic example of Jesus' rebuke occurred when merchants turned the temple into a store and profited from the poor and the pray-ers. Jesus made a whip out of cords and went after them, "scatter[ing] the coins of the money changers and overturn[ing] their tables. To those who sold doves he said, 'Get these out of here! How dare you turn my Father's house into a market!'" (See John 2:15–16.)

Should a pastor take a whip and go after his deacons, or call the men in his church dull-headed or snakes and vipers? Probably not! But, by all means, the wise pastor follows—to the letter—Jesus' example when he interacts with the women of the congregation.

HOW DO WOMEN WANT THEIR PASTORS TO RELATE TO THEM?

Women offer some concrete suggestions as to how they want to be treated by their pastors. Today's Christian woman wants her pastor to:

Value Her as a Person

A California woman writes: "Fortunately my current pastor of six years, and my former pastor of twenty-six years, both value women, and treat us with the same care, respect, and love that our Savior would."

A Tennessee woman explains: "Women make decisions differently than men. Let me use a 'knives' analogy. A man's brain is more like a hatchet, whereas a woman's is like a Swiss army knife—where many different thoughts are brought into consideration when making a decision. Be sure to involve women in the process of making important decisions, and value their participation."

Another writes: "I'd like for my pastor to know me and call me by name!"

An Oregon woman writes: "A minister who is strong in his faith will be more open to a woman's opinion. A woman's opinion is as valid as a man's—if that opinion is godly, carefully thought out, and comes after much prayer."

"My pastor is up to date on the trends of women and their needs," writes another. "We women need to be valued in churches, for our spiritual maturity and wisdom—provided, that is, that we are truly mature and are displaying the life that Christ asks of us."

From Tennessee: "Women are fellow image-bearers of God. We are, however, uniquely made, with particular abilities in the area of nurturing. Encourage us to use our gifts. Ask us our opinions. Be aware that we can greatly enhance the communication and compassion within a church community."

From Minnesota: "So many precious women need help. For many women, a pastor is kind of like God. I see women in all different situations, and when a pastor knows her name and values her as a person, it means so much to her. All women are special ... no one above the other."

From Washington state: "We need validation for ourselves and our ministry from the pastoral and elder leadership. If we are involved in leadership in a women's ministry, we need to know that the male leadership finds the ministry valuable. Show us our value by asking about our ministries, listening to us, and giving us opportunities to share our vision with the church and with the other leadership teams."

Encourage Her

An Alabama single mother of two writes: "There aren't enough encouragers today for the younger women of the church. They sometimes feel overwhelmed by the world and need special encouragement just to make it through the next day or week."

A South Carolina woman describes her pastor: "Our pastor is sufficiently versed in encouraging women. We are blessed to have him."

"Women need to be encouraged and assured they are doing what is right," writes a young woman from Pennsylvania. "We can sometimes be emotional people and we need to know we are on the right track. In the African-American community, the pastor is like a father figure to many young people—especially young girls. Encourage them, for sometimes the pastor is the only positive male influence in a young lady's life."

Another responds: "I need your prayers, encouragement, and support, and I will, in turn, pray for you, encourage you, and give you my support."

Appreciate Her

"Please, Pastor," writes a Virginia woman, "acknowledge my contributions. Proverbs 3:27 says 'don't withhold good from him to whom it is due.' Genuine appreciation will oil the machinery of our church fellowship."

Another acknowledges: "Women like to be told they are appreciated. Each of us would love to be thought of as loving, sensitive, knowledgeable, spiritual human beings, better each day, in every way."

"I need some confirmation, an 'atta girl' sometimes. I feel stretched out, sometimes even used," confesses an Oklahoma woman.

Another woman explains: "We need to be accepted and appreciated as co-ministers in the church, that is to say, equal in acceptance and expectation."

A woman from Oregon advises: "Pastor, be consistent. Be patient. Appreciate us for our unique ability to flourish and bring joy, laughter, and love to the church body."

Another says: "Don't be afraid of women. Don't be afraid of our emotions. That's the way God made us. Don't look at us as just something you have to put up with, like a toothache. Embrace us and encourage us to grow! We women have much to offer, and we need to be encouraged!"

Writes a woman from New England: "Pastor, be sensitive to and tolerant of a woman's opinions, lifestyle, and personality. Please appreciate today's Christian women and the heavy responsibilities they deal with on a daily basis."

"Sometimes pastors seem to be at a loss when it comes to dealing with the diverse lives we women lead," writes another. "We are wives, mothers, singles, grandmothers, stepmothers. We are cooks and caretakers and sisters. We are daughters, in-laws, friends, and confidants. If single, we are often babysitters, trip takers, helpers, and 'ask-her-she's-not-busy-errand-runners.' We are choir members, Sunday school teachers or members, committee members, prayer warriors, and organizers/implementers of various programs and projects. We are neighbors, cheerleaders to those who need encouragement, an ear for listening, and a heart for burdens.... We have cleaned out our pantries and closets to supply for those in dire need. Thankfully, we could do that and have been blessed by God for our efforts. We still feel the need, however, to be recognized and appreciated as a valuable resource in our churches. Yes, we are fallible. No, we are not perfect. To God be the glory for all the opportunities we have been given. We love him, and that's the reason we are still here."

Listen to Her

"I need a place to verbalize what I'm dealing with," says a Mississippi woman. "Verbalizing helps me resolve issues, and many times, by being allowed to verbalize, the solution becomes clear. But even if I don't immediately see a solution, I'll be emotionally helped just to be heard. So allow me to struggle. Struggle, in and of itself, is not necessarily bad. Please don't feel responsible, first and foremost, to 'fix it.'"

Another writes: "I admire the minister who takes time for women, looks them in the eye, and listens to them. So many times women say to me: 'I cannot believe my pastor took time with me. I am just a nobody in the church.'"

"We are serious about living Christian lives as mothers and workers outside the church," explains one woman. "Please listen to us when we share what God is doing in our lives, and where we believe we will be most effective as church workers. Hear us when we tell you about things in the church that need to change."

Get Acquainted with Her, Seek to Know Her, and Be Aware of Her Needs

One woman admits: "My present pastor shows a fine relationship with women in his church. He has become acquainted with the women in his church, and he preaches and pastors to them with a unique awareness of their needs."

"I wish I shared more of myself with my pastor," an Indiana woman confesses. "He is a wonderful, well-educated man. I feel free to come to him with any problem or praise, but I don't think he really *knows* me. I don't let him in close enough to see me, the *real* me. It is not him ... it's me that's the problem."

"I would like my pastor to know and love his members and they, in turn, to know, appreciate, and love him," another woman admits. "Be compassionate to families and suffering people in the church, and the less fortunate ones. Be an encourager. Be mission-minded."

A North Carolina woman wants her pastor "to know his flock. If he gets to know his flock, then his job will be more manageable. I want him to know my family's needs, be able to feed us from the Word, and reach out to each and every member of our church family. I believe the more you get to know someone, the more comfortable you become at sharing and caring. Just like our relationship with Christ."

"Basically," writes a New York woman, "I want my pastor to personally know the women in his church, not just the men, but the women and their children."

Another writes: "Women are great supporters of the church—not only with their gifts, but more importantly with their prayers."

"Understand that women often come to church with past hurts that color present-day situations," a California woman explains. "Men and women are different in their created natures. Often that nature is distorted by childhood events or patterns that destroy. In such cases, a woman's spiritual life—her journey with God—can be affected. Seek to understand who she is and why she is that way."

Understand and Acknowledge Her Relationships with Others

A Mississippi woman writes: "Know that I am almost always going to view problems/situations/opportunities in our church through the lens of relationships, and especially, family relationships. How church programs/problems impact my family will be dominant in my emotional response to those issues. Also, please know that besides the immediate problem, I have already extrapolated the consequences of the issue out to the third and fourth generation; I've already thought about how this issue will affect my future grandchildren."

From Georgia: "Pastor, women are not like men. Men and women alike have swallowed the feminist lie that there is essentially no difference between the two. We women need other women—to confide in, to chat with, to pray with, to cry and laugh with—far more than men do."

View Her as an Individual

A Texas survey reveals: "There are so many types of women in the church. There are those who are genuinely there to seek the Lord and to be in fellowship with other believers. Then there are those who are there strictly out of obligation and tradition. They feel they owe it to someone to be in church every Sunday. And some feel they just must continue the church tradition, since the entire family has always gone to church. Please, Pastor, don't put women into categories, but see us as unique individuals with varied and special talents!"

"Know that men and women *think* differently," writes another. "But women don't all think alike either. Varying educational levels and religious backgrounds affect the way the women think."

Show Interest and Participate (When Possible) in Her Ministry's Events/Activities

"My pastor's preaching/teaching and leadership are very appreciated as strong/truthful and challenging," writes a Colorado woman. "I would appreciate his presence at events the congregation sponsors. Our pastor seems to be a little shy, but his involvement outside worship services could strengthen our feelings for him."

A Michigan woman writes: "I'd like our pastor to visit our women's groups from time to time. This will let us know he is interested in what we do, how we think—and in general, what we are about."

Be Honest with Her

A Minnesota woman writes: "I want my pastor to correct the women of the church who get 'out of line' in the same way he would correct a man of the church who gets 'out of line.'"

"This might sound strange," writes an Alabama woman, "but I always wish that pastors would be more frank with women in the church. I've found that some pastors are afraid to speak plainly with a female in their church."

Another asks: "Will you be honest with me, Pastor? Honesty at all times keeps everyone happier."

Honor Her Confidences

A New Hampshire woman asks "her pastor to hold her conversations in confidence when she comes to him for counsel, comfort, or advice, and not to refer to them in any way, especially in public."

Understand and Consider a Woman's Life Stages

A woman from Virginia writes: "I believe pastors could counsel, encourage, and help women much more effectively if they had an understanding about the normal, common life stages that women go through. Consider how each stage of a woman's life—from early adulthood to her elderly years—presents different physical and spiritual challenges to her, as well as opportunities for her."

An Alabama pastor's wife acknowledges: "I wish pastors understood the unique ways God has made women to function: physically, mentally, spiritually, and emotionally. Pastor, take a close look at the women in your church, and try to understand the various changes and seasons in their lives."

I've listed only a few of the many ways today's women in the church hope pastors will relate to them. In all these ways, and others, Jesus ministered to the women of his own day. Of course, women understand that a pastor's time and energy—like their own—are both valuable and limited. Therefore, they suggest the pastor enlist their help in better understanding and ministering to the women in his church.

PASTORS, ENCOURAGE THE WOMEN IN YOUR CHURCH TO HELP YOU!

Women in the church can help a pastor better minister to the female congregants in many ways. They can:

1. Inform him about what is happening in the church's women's ministries and other areas of the church where women meet, greet, fellowship, and talk.
2. Keep him abreast of what is happening to the women in the community outside the church, and suggest ways he can minister to them.
3. Help him to better understand women and their common life-stages.
4. Seek him out when they sense a problem (or potential problem) in the church that involves the women.
5. Help him know how to best encourage, affirm, reassure, love, appreciate, and value the women in his congregation.
6. Make their personal needs known to him (or a church staff member or a women's ministry leader/director), and not suffer alone and in silence.
7. Help him learn the names of women in the congregation, as well as the names of their family members.
8. Help him understand how he can help church women grow spiritually through his sermons, church programs, events, etc.

Women also tell me that the pastor's wife can be a tremendous asset in helping her husband better understand the women in his congregation and minister to them. (Don't assume, however, that a pastor's wife has the time, energy, or willingness to do this. Enlist her help only after she volunteers it!)

A longtime minister's wife from Kentucky writes beautifully about her own life and role as a pastor's wife: "Since I have been a pastor's wife for sixty-one years, I have always tried to help my husband know as much as possible about the women who were active in the church. He was always interested in their personal lives, and he let them know that. I sensed that they needed a pastor to connect with and feel that they could come to him in their problems and in their joys. They always knew he would listen to them, and he would recognize them for their contribution as individuals. He always said that if there was a detailed job to be done, the women of the church would be the ones to get it done!"

I personally know this pastor and his lovely wife. And they have proved to be quite a ministerial team!

SURVEY SUMMARY

Today's Christian woman wants her pastor to know that:

- Jesus treated women with respect, dignity, forgiveness, affirmation, love, honor, kindness, compassion, tenderness, understanding, care, and concern. He gives today's pastors excellent examples to follow as they interact with, relate, and minister to the women in their church.

- Throughout the Gospels, Scripture shows that Jesus related—with his words and his actions—to men and women in different ways.

- She wants her pastor to value her as a person, to encourage and appreciate her, to listen to her when she speaks, to get acquainted with her, seek to know her, and be aware of her needs. She also wants him to understand and acknowledge her relationships with others, to view her as an individual, to show interest and participate (when possible) in her ministry's events and activities, to be honest with her, honor her confidences, and to consider her life-stages.

- She offers to help her pastor better understand the women in his church, to alert him of their individual needs, and to aid him as he seeks to minister to them as Jesus himself reached out to women in his ministry.

PART 5

WOMEN'S PERCEPTIONS OF CHURCH LIFE

CHAPTER 11

"PASTOR, WE HAVE SOME PROBLEMS IN OUR CHURCH"

Clothe yourselves with compassion, kindness, humility, gentleness, and patience. Bear with each other and forgive whatever grievances you may have against one another. Forgive as the Lord forgave you. And over all these virtues put on love, which binds them all together in perfect unity. Let the peace of Christ rule in your hearts, since as members of one body you were called to peace.

The apostle Paul, Colossians 3:12–15

I RECEIVED LITERALLY HUNDREDS of responses from women who are concerned about pressing problems in their churches. If you have served in a church leadership position for any period of time, you know it's hard to avoid problems; indeed, one doesn't enter into a church leadership position if the goal is to avoid problems and conflict.

If I asked you to come up with a list of what you think are the most common problems raised by women in the church, I wonder how closely your list would match what I found from my interviews across the country. (My guess is you could name quite a few.) In this chapter I invite you to join me in considering what I discovered. Perhaps some of what follows will resonate with you.

Specific concerns—eight to be exact—kept repeating themselves on survey after survey. To fully address these particular problems, I surely would need the space of a book—not just a single chapter—but I'll do my best to at least describe each and then let the women I surveyed speak for themselves.

PROBLEM #1: WORKING SEPARATELY

Men and women working separately rather than working together in ways that benefit the entire church body.

When church committees team both men and women, each gender brings valuable insights and needed perspectives to the issues or projects being considered. In New Testament times, men and women—who both made up the body of Christ—worked together for the benefit of the entire body. Paul writes clearly: "Just as each of us has one body with many members, and these members do not all have the same function, so in Christ we who are many form one body, and each member belongs to all the others" (Romans 12:4–5).

Yet women tell me that ideal New Testament union is not always happening in churches today.

An Alabama woman writes: "I sense that many pastors today don't recognize or use the expertise and capabilities of women. Some of the more active committees (building, finance, personnel, etc.) may have only one 'token' woman, if any—though numerous qualified women (realtors, bankers, corporate marketing, or human resources people) are eager to serve."

Another writes: "A woman can know as much, or more, about economics and investments than a male Wall Street broker! She can also chair and participate in important church committees with efficiency and skill. Give her a chance to serve!"

From Virginia: "I wish pastors understood the importance of men and women working together. Beginning in the teen years, males and females could discover—with a pastor's guidance—how to relate fully to each other, and work well together in life and ministry. All the separate men's and women's ministries may serve a good function in the church today, but in the end they should enable both genders to express the image of God together—mutually and intentionally—before a polarized world. Men's and women's individual ministry groups should not be deemed successful if they reinforce *separateness* rather than *unity*."

From Missouri: "Women's voices need to be heard on committees, planning teams, etc. But few women in my church are given the opportunity. Pastors must often be proactive and purposely seek out capable women to serve in decision-making positions where they can make a contribution and a difference."

From Arkansas: "Women should be included in decisions about how the church operates. Most of the decisions in my church are made by men. If women had a greater input in the operations of the church, I believe our church would grow in membership and service to the Lord."

From Oregon: "While we want to be sensitive to the biblical leadership structure of our church, we desire to be asked for input at a meaningful level. I believe it could save the church leadership much grief if they also included female perspectives."

A women's ministry director writes: "When women are left out of participating in making critical ministry decisions, churches often leave women's ministry needs unaddressed and unmet."

Several women expressed the practical need to voice their opinions on church building/designing/planning boards and committees:

"One area of my church, used for group meetings where refreshments are needed, was designed without female input. It has no food service facilities. The nearest kitchen sink and running water are located on a different level and accessible only by stairs."

Another writes: "Our church kitchen has zero lights in it! Perhaps that's because no women were invited into the meetings when the blueprints were discussed."

Another writes: "A committee of men in our church are in the process of creating/designing a children's playground—without a mom's advice, ideas, and creativity! It's no wonder they are frustrated and getting nowhere."

An Illinois church council member tells how she has learned to operate more successfully on an all-male council: "I've learned that if I want the male pastors and staff to hear what I'm proposing, I must write it out in outline form. I've learned to always make my final point the most important point. I request a written response to my requests by a certain date. I list both the pros and cons to a proposal so the men won't feel 'strong-armed' into accepting it. I find I get more respect from the men if I've carefully thought things through, keep a low profile, and avoid teary responses."

Women tell me that they often purposely change their ingrained work and personal habits in order to communicate more effectively with male committee members and gain their respect. But, they say, voicing their opinion, and being heard, is worth the effort.

Dr. Sarah Sumner writes that a team made up of women and men must have at least two components: "unity in purpose and commitment to a group dynamic." And that the three main attitudes needed in teamwork are: "respect (to show 'esteem, deference, or honor'), humility, and love."[1]

She writes: "I believe the answer is for church leaders to pray and cast vision. Pastors can pray for God to help them paint a picture and model it in the staff and ministry teams, of brotherly-sisterly love in Christ."[2]

Teamwork, even among churched Christians, requires the qualities Paul mentions in Colossians 3—especially kindness, humility, gentleness, patience, love—"which binds them all together *in perfect unity*"—and peace—"since as members of *one body* [we are] called to *peace*" (Colossians 3:12–15, my emphasis).

PROBLEM #2: LACK OF RESPECT

Men not respecting the different ways women plan, implement, and work.

A Texas woman writes: "Women often make decisions in ways very different than men. We still accomplish the same goal, but we often arrive at it through processes that men neither understand nor tolerate very well. But, regardless of how we 'get there,' we still make valuable contributions to committees."

Men must understand that often women create and think differently than they do. The response from this Texas woman made me think of how differently men and women actually do come to the same, or similar conclusions.

Not to unfairly stereotype today's men and women, nor make across-the-board generalizations, let me share some insights into the different behaviors of men and women.

Bill and Pam Farrel, authors of *Men Are Like Waffles, Women Are Like Spaghetti*, write: "Before [a woman] looks for solutions, she interacts with each part of her life and experiences the appropriate emotion of each issue."[3]

I too have found this insight to be true. Given a woman's relational nature, and her need to verbalize every aspect and consider every potential possibility of every action, a committee meeting might last indefinitely. Some experts believe it has to do with the number of nerve cells in a woman's brain, and how they enable a woman to use both the left and right sides of her brain simultaneously. Men's brains, however, lack the vast number of "spaghetti-like" nerve cells that women possess. Their brains are more like "waffles," in that men think in separate little blocks, or boxes, using only the left side of the brain. "We find it amusing," write the Farrels, "that even when it comes to the use of the brain, women connect both sides while men keep it as simple as possible by using only one side."[4]

Regardless of the accuracy of this theory, one thing's for sure: the business style of a committee meeting made up only of spaghetti (women) and the business style of a committee meeting made up only of waffles (men) will differ significantly! Put men and women together into the decision-making committee meeting, blend in a good mixture of kindness and patience, and the goal accomplished will be better balanced because both genders brought their God-given gifts to the project.

PROBLEM #3: LACKING NEW OPPORTUNITIES

Women lacking new opportunities to serve the church in nontraditional women's roles.

For years, women have devotedly served churches in some fairly typical areas of ministry, particularly: with child/nursery care, as children's Sunday school teachers, with choir and music programs, with food services and as church dinner coordinators, with worship service decorating and flower arranging, as women's ministry directors, with missions outreach projects, and with clothes and food pantries for the needy. Women call these jobs the "traditional" roles of women in the church (some argue, however, these roles became "traditional" only after the third century).

While many women are content with serving in these capacities, many others want to be involved in the same kind of church roles Paul himself called women to fill. Consider some of Scripture's influential women, such as *Priscilla*, who, with her husband, Aquila—"fellow workers in Christ Jesus" (Romans 16:3)—helped launch Apollos's ministry (Acts 18:24–26); and *Chloe* (1 Corinthians 1:11), *Nympha* (Colossians 4:15), and others.

"Pastor," writes a South Carolina woman, "know that women are available and qualified to serve on administration boards, nominating committees, and places other than in the nursery and children's Sunday school classes. While children's programs are a blessing to us, we are in a 'rut,' and we want to do more."

A Florida woman writes: "We are more diverse than anyone realizes. The church's *culture* keeps women in traditional roles—*not the Bible*. It saddens me to see women given more freedom to do important work *in the world* today than *in the church*. I think Jesus accepted women more in his time than the Christian culture does in ours."

"Women are vital to the health of our church!" says an Oregon woman. "If you don't have women connected, involved, and active within every area of the church, the overall health of the church will suffer."

Another comments: "Women in my church seem to be 'politely tolerated.' They are sometimes invited to participate on committees, but the men make all the decisions. Men hold the power in the church. I wish I could figure out how to exercise influence in a way that is nonthreatening to men. Then, perhaps, they might include me."

Another writes: "God designed men and women to 'complete' each other — not just in marriage, but in the life of the church."

A Tennessee woman writes: "Churches need women on their staffs to include a woman's perspective, and to represent the female side of the membership. An all-male staff just cannot relate to the women as well as a female staff member can."

A number of women, who served the church in women's traditional roles, felt that the congregation often overlooked or failed to value their hard work.

A Florida woman acknowledges: "The traditional ministries of many women in our church often go unnoticed. I encourage pastors to realize, and recognize, the huge amount of work women do in behind-the-scenes roles."

Another writes: "I wish our pastor knew how hard our women work, and how much time they spend to get God's work done in the church."

"During its early years," writes Linda Hartz Rump, "Christianity taught a spiritual unity that at least potentially mitigated the harshness of Roman law, in which women were considered non-citizens with no legal rights. Inequality was everywhere in this system.... Over against this culture, the ideal of the early church is captured in the words of Paul, 'Be subject to one another in the fear of Christ' (Ephesians 5:21). And women did ... gain some status 'in Christ,' [and filled] key roles within the church."[5]

PROBLEM #4: SECOND-CLASS CITIZENS

Women not taken seriously in church, and often made to feel like second-class citizens.

In this category, the sheer number of survey responses proved overwhelming! They poured in from women of all ages and stages of life, both single and married, from all around the country. Some women expressed sadness. Others expressed anger.

From Georgia: "We women are serious about the work we do for God and the church. We aren't just 'airheads'!"

From Tennessee: "Pastors, take us seriously! We serve in vital roles and leadership positions in society. We should also be playing a vital role in our local congregations!"

From Florida: "Women in my church are taken less seriously than their male counterparts. Men in our church tend to think we women are 'flighty and emotional.' What's wrong with showing emotions? Why not embrace this side of women rather than eschew it?"

From Oregon: "Pastor, I'm not out to preach your sermons, but, on behalf of the church, I have some serious things to discuss with you. Know that as a woman I can often bring things to the table that men might not see. And from a different perspective than most males. Together, men and women can do better, more balanced work for God's kingdom. Nothing happens when we are isolated, or at odds, or struggling with each other. After all, we are created in the image of God, both 'male and female.' When one of us is weak, the other can be strong. And vice versa."

From Alabama: "Pastor, don't discount my observations and insight into Scripture just because I am a woman. I can hear from God too. I want to be taken seriously when I have a point to make."

From Georgia: "I am an adult with worthy ideas and sound opinions. I do not like feeling marginalized by the men in the church simply because I am a woman. I want my ideas and opinions given fair consideration, and the opportunity to impact the church in positive ways, without having to apologize for being a woman. Pastor, I can do more than sing and serve food."

From California: "Pastor, when I appear to *take charge* and express my ideas, I am not trying to be 'unsubmissive' and 'in control.' I believe that if women were *always* silent in the church, many concerns would remain unaddressed and many projects would never be realized."

From Illinois: "In many churches, women are simply not taken seriously, no matter how, or in what ways, God has gifted us."

From Iowa: "Pastor, when you address me, address me as a whole person—not just one half of my husband. Please take me as seriously as you do him!"

Women today want their pastors, as well as the men in their churches, to take them seriously—both their words and their work. When they don't, women tell me they often feel like second-class citizens in church. Numerous women complained about feeling "second class," so I looked up the word in my dictionary. Webster's defines the word as "pertaining to a class next below the first; second-rate; mediocre."

Three women write:

"I wish the pastor, and men in my church, would not treat me, and the other women, like second-class citizens. We are also capable people."

"Women are not second class in the family of God! After all, God thought a woman first-class enough to carry Jesus—the Word of God—inside her womb!"

"The church is a *covenant* community, and women are not second-class citizens."

PROBLEM #5: AGE DISCRIMINATION

Age discrimination against women in the church.

While only two elderly women complained about age discrimination in the church, I feel it is important they be heard. No doubt, pastors are aware that age discrimination may increase in the church in future years. Experts estimate that by 2030, the number of people older than sixty-five will have grown to 70 million (a 125 percent increase from 1990), including a doubling of those aged eighty-five years and older (to 8.9 million).[6]

A widow from Maine writes: "Because I am elderly doesn't mean I can't still be effective in church work. It's true that some elderly women have health problems and can't serve in various church capacities. But I am in good health and energetic. I hunger to serve my church in significant ways."

Another widow writes: "Please make the church's older women feel loved and valued. Ask the church's young families to visit them."

It's interesting that throughout Scripture, God constantly shows his love, special attention, and deep appreciation for the aged, particularly for elderly widows. He often uses their examples to teach valuable lessons to others. Consider Naomi (Ruth 4:15); the special widow in Zarephath (1 Kings 17:8–16; also Luke 4:24–26); Anna, the insightful prophetess (Luke 2:36–38); the widow at Nain (Luke 7:12–15); and the generous widow (Luke 21:1–4).

While some complaints of discrimination came from elderly women, most came from *single women*—both young, middle aged, and older—who had either never married, or who had been divorced or widowed. (We will look at this type of discrimination in the next chapter.)

PROBLEM #6: MEN AND LEADERSHIP

Problems with men regarding church leadership and church work.

Women today complain about three distinctive types of men in the church:

Dominating Men

An Alabama woman writes: "Deacons in our church are given too much power. They control too much. They don't consult the congregation, they just act."

A Florida woman confesses: "The male superiority attitude has driven me from my church."

A Georgia woman writes: "I personally see too many pastors, and other men in the church, with an attitude of superiority. They act like God's *man* is never wrong, and he should never be questioned. I've been in this situation twice, and I know firsthand that these churches never grow."

Another declares: "I wish our deacons would remember that this is *God's* church, not the deacons' church!"

"The church is still a male-dominated arena," writes another. "There's simply too much power given to too few members!"

Weak, Ineffective Men

"The church today lacks strong male leadership," writes an Oklahoma woman. "It has been my experience that responsibility to execute church programming falls primarily upon the ladies of the church, but without proper leadership/guidance. Having all of the responsibility to execute church programming, but no opportunity to participate in decisions that affect programming, is frustrating for us. It usually results in feeling 'used' by the church leadership rather than a feeling of inclusion and appreciation."

A Tennessee woman requests: "Pastors, please help raise up male leaders. Women crave to have strong men as leaders."

A Louisiana woman writes: "Churches today lack good Christian men who are willing to do the work of the Lord—especially leadership work with boys. Pastors, tell men they need to 'step up' and mentor young boys. When men won't do it, the church's women are forced into these roles. The lack of Christian men in our churches today leads young boys into believing that religion is a women's thing, and not a man's."

"Pastors, tell men to become strong spiritual leaders in their families and in our churches. We need more dedicated men who will pray, witness, and work with children. It seems like the women are pulling most of the workload at church." (California)

"Some men at my church seem 'threatened' by strong, hardworking women. My theory is—if men were 'on fire' and ministering like Jesus, they wouldn't feel threatened by a 'woman on fire.' It's like the woman at the well (John 4:1–42, especially verses 31–34). She was 'getting the whole town saved' and brought to Jesus, while the disciples worried about what they were going to eat!" (Minnesota)

"We're lacking our men's influence in church today. The men need to be encouraged in their Christian manhood, as well as taught and mentored to become strong disciples of Christ. Boys especially need to be trained by the church in every aspect of manhood." (Illinois)

Another writes: "Weak, ineffective men weaken a church. When men 'drop back' and fail to take responsibilities in church, the women must take over more and more jobs."

"For whatever reason, the men in our church have stopped taking leadership roles. Why, I am not sure. Maybe it's because it's just one less thing they have to do. I know our women are more than capable of leading the church, but it really concerns me that I see fewer and fewer men actively involved in the church. I think it's so important to have strong male leadership!" (Alabama)

"I believe the number one problem women face in churches today is the lack of male leadership." (Tennessee)

"In my church, we women are the ones who mostly volunteer for service in the church, as well as raising the children, and encouraging spiritual relationships among our members. It would be so helpful if the church recognized this fact, and gave our wonderful men the encouragement they need to become our leaders." (Missouri)

"Uncommitted" Men

A woman from Maine complains: "Pastor, women are doing most of the work in my church, including ministries, prayer, outreach, etc. I am becoming frustrated with men who want to be leaders and who want respect, but don't study the Scriptures and don't 'walk the walk.' How can women respect that?"

A Tennessee woman writes: "Women are essential in the life of the church, but they are not supposed to hold the church together all by themselves. When men become 'members only' and leave all the work up to the women in the church, women take on too many responsibilities while the men just 'warm the pews.' The women of the church then must become 'too much Martha' and 'not enough Mary'!"

"Men need to help us teach Sunday school classes! There are twice as many women teachers in our church as male teachers," writes another.

"I am tired," confesses a thirty-seven-year-old mother from North Carolina. "The women in my church carry most of the workload. Where are the men? I am frustrated that the men in my church won't stand up and fill more roles and provide the church with strong leadership."

An Alabama woman writes: "I think women take on so much work in the church because the men won't step up and say 'yes' to spiritual leadership. The women at my church crave for men to lead the congregation and be spiritual examples."

Another writes: "Over the years, the women of our church have almost singlehandedly held the church together during lean, hard times. Why? Because, sadly, most of the men in our church community are not committed to Jesus or to the church."

One woman asks and then answers: "What's the number one problem for Christian women today? Well, to put it bluntly: quality, committed, Jesus-loving *men*! Or the lack thereof. As women grow and become strong in their faith, men fall behind with apathetic attitudes and leave an ever-widening gap in the church. I wish pastors would teach men to become the men of God they are called to be—and, I believe, the type of men they *really want to become*."

A New England woman raises an interesting point: "Why are women seemingly more hungry, and more willing to pursue their relationship with God, and be involved in Bible studies than men?" she asks. "Sometimes my heart cries out, 'Where are the men? To be leaders, teachers, mentors, prayer warriors?' Someone has said, 'If there's vacuum, a woman will fill it.' I wonder if that is what has happened in the church, and as a result men have stepped back? Have we created a catch-22? Are the preaching and leadership styles such that they appeal to women more than men?"

From Tennessee: "We have a dearth of male leadership in our nation. The lack of effective male Christian leaders is obvious—in the church as well as in the home. Pastors need to help raise up male leaders—real 'statesmen'—for the sake of our homes, our churches, and our government."

From New York: "There is a significant absence of men in the current evangelical church, and we women are frustrated by this. I'd like to see ministers become more intentional about discipleship and the mentoring of men in the church. Women are tired of going to church without their husbands, and are frustrated that ministers are not reaching out to men and helping them grow in their relationship with Christ."

From New Jersey: "My church would have very little ministry or work done without women. The men most often do nothing more than show up on an occasional Sunday morning when they are summoned for their business advice and/or leadership decisions."

A pastor's wife writes: "If it weren't for the hardworking women in our church, nothing would get done, and classes wouldn't have teachers."

One woman complains: "Women in my church do more than fix a meal or plan a church fellowship. They drive the bus, fix the plumbing, and mow the grass! Find the men, and spread the workload!"

A Kentucky woman writes: "Our women are 'burning out' from all the work! Please, Pastor, put the men in the kitchens and classrooms with the women, and both share the work. Let's all work together to do the jobs that need to be done!"

Says an Illinois woman: "In my church, women are expected to do everything—especially those jobs men consider insignificant. Men do nothing in the church that requires really hard work. In my youth, the excuse was that women were home all day and men had jobs. Never mind that my mother probably worked harder than my father, who never went to church. Today, women also work jobs, and they are still expected to take care of home and children, plus do the hard jobs in the church."

PROBLEM #7: COMPETITION AMONG WOMEN

Competition among women, "catfighting," cliques, and women behaving badly.

Let me reacquaint you with two Christian women in the church in Philippi: Euodia and Syntyche. Paul notes that these two hardworking women "have contended at my side in the cause of the gospel," and that their names "are in the book of life" (Philippians 4:3). For some reason, however, Euodia and Syntyche argued between themselves. So Paul writes: "I plead with Euodia and I plead with Syntyche to agree with each other in the Lord" (4:2). Paul also enlists the aid of a "loyal yokefellow," as well as "Clement and the rest of my fellow workers," to help Euodia and Syntyche to get along with each other (4:3).

I was surprised by the number of women who told me they knew women in today's churches who often hurt each other, "catfight," compete with one another, and fall victim to the "Euodia-Syntyche syndrome." Surely, Christ's church is no place for women competing against each other, and women behaving badly! Didn't Paul write that there should be no division in the body (1 Corinthians 12:25)? Women might not necessarily "like" each other's offensive habits and peculiar ways, but they must "love one another" in Christ (John 13:34–35), and be careful what they say to and about each other (Ephesians 4:29). They are to put away all "bitterness, rage and anger, brawling and slander, along with every form of malice. Be kind and compassionate to one another, forgiving each other" (4:31–32), and minister to one another's needs (Matthew 25:40).

Listen to some of the survey responses I received about this problem:

"Many women in my church carry heartache because of the critical words of other women in the church." (Mississippi)

"Women in the church can be cruel. Pastor, break up their little 'cliques' and preach messages about love and kindness." (Tennessee)

"Territorialism within groups is a real problem among women in my church. Their in-fighting for control and recognition is displayed through the development of cliques, various positioning for responsibilities in the church, and selfish desires for the 'limelight.' And it's destructive to the women and to the church. I have never heard of a pastor directly addressing these female 'catfighting' and 'territorialism' issues before the church. I'm sure women would perceive such a message to be negative and meant to 'single them out.' But it might be helpful!" (Alabama)

"Unfortunately, many women I know 'compete' with each other instead of 'complete' each other. I believe the problem can be resolved when we come into one accord with Christ and with one another." (Georgia)

"I think it would be beautiful to see pastors encouraging women to work in cooperation with one another, and not in competition. I think jealousy and strife stem from what the world calls 'making it to the top,' and 'keeping up with the Joneses.' When women bring the world's mentality into the church, the Devil causes us to lose our common spiritual focus. If pastors knew that gossip, jealousy, envy, and backbiting were serious issues in today's church, he would point women to the Word to resolve their issues, forgive each other, and be forgiven. He would help women learn more ways to encourage each other and celebrate their mutual love for Christ." (Texas)

Another woman writes: "Sometimes women lure other women into our churches by painting a picture of love and harmony, and giving a pseudo-snapshot of what Christian female relationships look like. Then, when women join, we either run them off with our bickering, or offend and hurt them with our cliques."

"I believe the primary challenge women face in the church today is competition among themselves," writes another. "The desire to be a better mom, a thinner woman, a greater cook and homemaker, a more loyal church member, etc., often drives women to compare themselves with other women. Competition happens when they find themselves lacking in some area. A subtle tension exists for women in the church to seek to impress each other by comparing their material possessions, accomplishments, quality of education, figure, husband's position, friendships, etc. Envy, jealousy, bitterness, backbiting, slander, and gossip can all stem from the negative competition among women."

Other women listed isolation, superficiality, fear, distrust, and low self-esteem as additional reasons women hurt each other and feel competitive.

A California woman writes: "Women don't seem to trust Christian women any more than they trust women outside the church. Women carry a mistrust of each other, and it prevents intimacy, even in the church—the safest place to find redemptive relationships. Women secretly despise and envy each other in regards to wealth, children, and men—even the closest relationships may be underscored by a wounded mistrust. I wish Christian women today better understood the 'sisterhood' available to them through God's grace, and learned to reach out with genuine love to one another."

Perhaps Paul addresses some of these women when he writes: "Do everything without complaining or arguing, so that you may become blameless and pure, children of God without fault in a crooked and depraved generation, in which you shine like stars in the universe" (Philippians 2:14–15).

PROBLEM #8: SECULARISM IN CHURCH

Secularism: the world's "foot" in the church's "door."

A Texas woman writes: "A lot of Christian women these days believe that in order to be 'the best woman possible,' they have to be independent, make a six-figure salary, look good, and drive a Lexus. We live in a 'flirty and thriving' world, and pastors could help us to see that our value is in God's Word—not in the world's definition of success."

From Maine: "Women today are given double messages from society and the church. There is a constant battle to stay in God's Word and God's will as we try to live in a society that doesn't care about our walk with God."

From Louisiana: "I see Christian women today seeking satisfaction in the wrong things. They've never been taught that the only true source of satisfaction is Christ."

"The number one problem Christian women today face," writes a single mom with two young children, "is that they have bought into the lies of our culture. I believe that too often the Christian church culture doesn't look much different from the secular culture. It's a shame."

"How is the church going to influence the world," asks one woman, "if the church has become just like the world?"

A woman writes from Oklahoma: "Christian women today are conforming themselves to secular standards of mind and heart rather than to biblical truth. Too many Christian women seek the world's things and pleasures and fail to seek God."

Another writes: "The church seems to be competing with the world by offering Hollywood-type entertainment during worship services, and the noisy 'rah rah' atmosphere of a high school pep rally. Women desperately need a word from God each week in a quiet worshipful place. Mature women in the faith need biblical substance. They prefer a contemplative environment. Today's church worship service has drowned out the voice of God. It's too much like the world. We want a place set apart to meet God!"

A Missouri mother says: "Whether our idols are money, children, body image, and/or career prestige, women today need to throw out the world's idols, put God back on the throne of our lives, and get our lives in spiritual balance."

Another asks: "Pastor, will you please help us become more godly in this ungodly world? The world is quickly creeping into our lives, and it's hard for today's Christian woman to remain godly. Our children come home from school with ungodly words and actions, and we feel frustrated trying to mold and make them into Christ-loving children."

A woman from Oklahoma believes that "women want their children to fit in with the world too much."

A Tennessee woman explains how hard it is for women to "live out what God's Word says in a world that is telling them to do the opposite. We try to stay connected to Christ in a world of distractions, but are continually failing to do so."

Another laments: "The church is starting to feel like 'big business' instead of the body of Christ."

Perhaps a woman from Mississippi offers the best defense against our struggle with secularism: "Women must find their identity in Christ! I believe women today search for their identity in everything, and everyone, except Christ. Many women place their identity in their job, or their husband's job, or their children, or their social status, etc. I've found that discovering who a woman is in Christ can be one of the most joyful, freeing, confidence-building things a woman can do. Christian women, as well as today's church pastors, must help women discover their identity in Christ, and we must begin with young women—adolescents, teens, and college-aged women."

Amen to that.

Today's Christian woman wants her pastor to know that:

- She yearns for men and women to work together in harmony in the church, so that together they might build up the body of Christ.
- Women and men often think, work, and solve problems in ways diverse and different from each other.
- She craves new opportunities to personally serve the church in capacities other than "traditional women's roles."
- She wants to be "taken seriously" in her church, and not be made to feel like a second-class citizen.
- She wants her church to eliminate age discrimination against elderly women.
- She needs her pastor to address problems regarding the leadership and work of men in the church.
- She craves intimacy and friendship among the women in the church, and yearns to eliminate competition, "catfighting," cliques, and other forms of un-Christlike behavior.
- She wants the world's "foot" removed from the church's "door." She wants to get secularism and society's pseudo-values out of the church.

CHAPTER 12

"PASTOR, WHERE DO SINGLES FIT INTO OUR CHURCH?"

> *I commend to you our sister Phoebe, a servant of the church in Cenchrea. I ask you to receive her in the Lord in a way worthy of the saints and to give her any help she may need from you, for she has been a great help to many people, including me.*
>
> **The apostle Paul, Romans 16:1 – 2**

A NUMBER OF SINGLE WOMEN responded to the survey. Most told me they felt they just didn't "fit" into their churches. They felt left out because they weren't married.

One never-married single attended her church on Christmas Eve. "My pastor asked all the families — one at a time — to walk forward and place an ornament on the Christmas tree," she writes. "Can you imagine how odd I felt as a single woman? I wish pastors would be more aware of, and more sensitive to, the feelings of their church's single women."

A Tennessee never-married single notes: "As single women, we feel like the forgotten group in the church. Singles feel lonelier in church than they feel out in the world."

Another single, newly divorced woman with no children writes: "Our church advertises its picnics and socials by telling members to 'bring your family.' I never feel invited or included in these events."

SCRIPTURE HONORS SINGLE WOMEN

Throughout Scripture, God appreciated, honored, and used single women to bring about his kingdom purposes. Consider the life and work of Miriam, Moses' sister (Micah 6:4); the Samaritan woman at Jacob's well (John 4:39–41); Mary, Jesus' friend (Luke 10:39, 42); Martha, Jesus' friend (10:38); Mary Magdalene (John 20:18); and Phoebe (Romans 16:1). These women were single and God valued them and used them in significant ways.

Yet the survey responses reveal that single women today (whether never married, divorced, or widowed) admit they often feel like second-class citizens because they aren't "paired with a man."

Some singles tell me that their pastors have even disallowed them ministry positions in the church—especially in leadership roles—because they aren't married.

Others say that often members of the congregation believe singles go to church only in order to meet a man—a "Mr. Right" whom they can marry—and that single women are considered "unwhole" or "incomplete" because they aren't married.

Many singles wonder if the church even values them and appreciates their involvement and contributions to church ministry.

DOES THE CHURCH APPRECIATE ITS SINGLES?

A young never-married North Carolina woman writes: "I wish my pastor would dress up like a woman and attend a church service! More than likely, without a spouse with him, he would be ignored. Being 'mate-less' is like being invisible in my church. I sometimes feel like an 'untouchable.'"

A single, divorced mother of two writes: "Although many of my fellow church members—both male and female—won't agree, I believe that what I say in church is just as important as what a married woman says."

A forty-year-old, never-married woman from Georgia writes: "My church doesn't have a clue what to do with its middle-aged single women! I feel like an 'alien' on Sunday mornings because of my age and single status."

Another writes: "Most single women in my church lead extremely productive lives outside of church! But, within the walls of the church, people in the congregation still look down on them."

A recently divorced, thirty-year-old woman writes: "Last Sunday evening I attended a concert at church. The bulletin contained a printed message that said women should keep silent in church or speak only through their husbands. I spent the whole evening wondering: 'Do I have a voice in church since I no longer have a husband?'"

A middle-aged widow complains: "I'm tired of church members asking me if I've met any 'eligible bachelors' at church! I don't come to church to meet a potential husband! I come to church to worship God!"

A young never-married woman writes: The singles program at my church seems only interested in matching up men and women, and getting them married. I feel like I'm on display there, and trying to pass some marriage-eligibility test!"

A twenty-two-year-old never-married woman comments: "Pastor, please know that I am interested in more than dating! I want to live a well-balanced life where Christ is the center. I also want to minister to a group of vivacious Christian adults who also want a Christ-centered life. My sole purpose is not to just wait for a good mate and get married!"

A longtime single, recently married woman from Texas writes: "I wish pastors would convince the single women in the church that it's okay to be single until God says 'get married.' I was single for forty-one years before I got married. I had lots of single friends who were desperately searching, seeking, and earnestly praying for 'Mr. Right.' For some reason, the congregation often makes single women believe that being married (and birthing a child) makes her a 'complete woman.' It doesn't! A woman is totally complete *in Christ*! Single women listen too much to the voices of society, and not nearly enough to God's voice. Tell them it's okay to be single!"

SINGLES IN THE UNITED STATES TODAY

Statistically speaking, did you know that:

- The number of single-person households is rapidly growing? "The number of single-person households in the U.S. grew 21 percent in the 1990s, eclipsing the growth rates for all other types of living arrangements."[1]
- "About 27.2 million Americans lived alone in 2000, accounting for about 26 percent of all households and about 9.7 percent of the overall U.S. population"?[2]
- "The nuclear family setup of two parents and their children is no longer the most common living arrangement in the United States ... [and that] in its place at the No. 1 spot is the 'single-adult' household"? "The strange new truth, according to census figures, is that the single largest chunk of American households now consists of people who live alone. No spouse or partner, no kids or other relatives, no roommate or boarder. Alone."[3]

- "Families consisting of breadwinner dads and stay-at-home moms now account for just one-tenth of all households"? And "married couples with kids, which made up nearly every residence a century ago, now total just 25 percent—with the number projected to drop to 20 percent by 2010, says the Census Bureau. By then, nearly 30 percent of homes will be inhabited by someone who lives alone."[4]
- "In 1950, just 9.3 percent of U.S. households consisted of people living alone"? "No wonder," writes one reporter, "the unmarried minority was viewed as *freakish* at the time!"[5]

Charles Colson writes about this surprising new trend. "Now, first let me say that it's important for Christians, when examining this trend, to avoid pointing fingers or acting as if singles are somehow inferior to married people.... Paul teaches in the New Testament, not everyone is called to be married."[6]

Women (and men) are single today for many reasons. Here are just a few. Some singles are called by God to be single, and don't want to marry. Some are invested entirely into ministry and careers and have decided to remain unmarried. Many singles are postponing marriage until later in life. Some are staying single because they are fearful of commitment and/or afraid of today's high divorce rates among Christians. Still others are having a hard time finding someone with whom they share common interests or want to marry. Many singles today are living together without getting married.

WHAT DOES THE INCREASING SINGLE STATUS MEAN FOR THE CHURCH?

The fact that the singles population in the United States is steadily increasing holds vast implications for government and educational institutions, legal systems, advertisers and retailers, the workplace, and so on. They are seriously discussing the potential implications, and busily preparing for the increase.

"Every church of every size has single adults," states Eileen Wright, an associate in the office of discipleship and family ministries at the Alabama Baptist State Board of Missions. "That doesn't necessarily mean every church needs a single adult ministry, but it does mean that churches need to think about single adults in their planning.... We need to be looking at singles with different eyes. Singles are viable, active people that run the whole gamut of ministries and opportunities."[7]

Should not the churches also be discussing this important demographic surge and preparing for it as well? I believe it should.

Today's Christian single woman wants her pastor to know that:

- Throughout Scripture, God appreciated, honored, and used single women to bring about his kingdom purposes.
- Single women today (whether they are never married, divorced, or widowed) often feel like they just don't fit into their local church, that they often feel like second-class citizens because they aren't "paired with a man."
- A woman—married or unmarried—is totally complete *in Christ*!
- The population of singles in the United States is growing in number.
- Paul teaches in the New Testament that not everyone is called to be married.
- Singles have many reasons for staying single.
- Churches need to give more thought to the single adults in their congregations.
- Singles have an important place in church ministry.

CHAPTER 13

"PASTOR, SHOULD WOMEN BE CHURCH LEADERS?"

> *Some follow a literal interpretation of certain biblical passages and make a case for the submission of women to men in the church.... They interpret Genesis 2 to mean that Eve was created to be Adam's helper and that ancient cultural pattern is applied universally to the present.... Others ... follow an egalitarian perspective. In Galatians 3:27–28, Paul wrote, "As many of you as are baptized into Christ have clothed yourselves with Christ. There is no longer Jew or Greek, there is no longer slave or free, there is no longer male and female, for all of you are one in Christ Jesus" (NRSV).*[1]

Sheri Adams

PASTOR, I WRITE THIS CHAPTER with "fear and trembling"—and with much prayer. Let me remind you again of my role in the creation of this book: I am merely the "messenger"! I realize I took a risk when I placed blank surveys into the hands of Christian women around the country, and asked them the question: "What do you want your pastor to know?" After receiving hundreds upon hundreds of responses, I now also realize that I take an even greater risk by compiling their candid opinions, views, insights, and criticisms into a publishable manuscript. I promised the women anonymity, and encouraged them to "speak" honestly and openly. And, Pastor, they did!

I painstakingly reviewed and recorded their responses and, in the end, I made some shocking discoveries. When Christian women voiced their opinions about women in church leadership positions—a topic they themselves brought up—each woman felt strongly in either one of two ways: They either *strongly* urged women to "obey the Bible" (their own words) and take subordinate positions in the church (subordinate to men—often referred to as "traditional women's roles"); or they *strongly* urged women to "step up to the plate" (their own words) and "lead" the church in the areas of speaking/praying in worship services, chairing committees, serving as deacons/elders, making church decisions, teaching men's (or mixed) classes, etc. Some women—especially those pursuing theological degrees—also wanted to preach, pastor, and become ordained.

Women on both sides were passionate about their opinions! There was no middle ground! No woman took a neutral position! It was entirely "either/or"!

In the end, I saw that each woman's view, each individual's strong—and often harsh and angry—opinion was based on two camps of criteria: what she had been taught by others (pastors, church, Sunday school teachers, parents, grandparents, friends, etc.) to believe about Scripture, *and* how she herself interpreted Scripture. I also found that these two issues moved beyond the walls of the church, and into the Christian home. What women believed about their God-given role in the church also applied to their roles as wives and mothers.

THE ISSUE BRINGS CONTROVERSY

I personally believe the issue of women in church leadership will never be solved or fully agreed upon by both sides. But one thing is for sure: mention women in church leadership, and (I can tell you from firsthand experience!) you are bound to stir up controversy.

On July 16, 1990, *Christianity Today* published an article titled: "Can We Talk?" in response to an earlier article in the magazine that profiled Roberta Hestenes, president of Eastern College. In the same issue, *CT* printed two advertisements—one from the Council on Biblical Manhood and Womanhood, and another from Christians for Biblical Equality. *CT* editors write: "It happens every time we publish something about Women in Leadership ... we get lots of (predictable) letters. If an article endorses women in leadership roles, many letters object and a few congratulate. If the article endorses a male hierarchy, many object and a few congratulate. Letters come from men and women alike."

Who writes these letters? "A certain percentage [are] from axe-grinders," but far more are from "serious-minded evangelicals who have strong beliefs on this subject and want to share them.... Many are filled with solid exegesis [and] others passionately marshal theological, philosophical, sociological, and psychological data. These are not harsh, unknown critics," they conclude, "but friends of *CT*."[2]

As you well know, interpretation of certain Scripture verses is causing "civil war" between women, as well as great adversity and division between men and women, churches and denominations. No doubt, you are already well-acquainted with these particular Scripture verses. I don't need to list them, and I certainly offer no personal opinion on their interpretation! You may have even memorized these "troublesome" passages. No doubt, at some time in your ministry, you've personally wrestled with them, and may have even preached them. You may still be struggling in trying to interpret them.

SOME AMAZING RESPONSES

One survey respondent quoted a paragraph from the pages of J. Lee Grady's book, *Twenty-Five Tough Questions about Women and the Church*. Grady writes: "Although women in the United States have civil freedom, equal rights in the workplace and the full protection of law, many church leaders continue to quench the fire that burns in our sisters. We deny them equal rights to participate in the life of the church, and we slam the door on opportunities for leadership. We encourage them to be passive, as if timidity were a virtue. We tell women who believe God has given them gifts of leadership, prophecy, pastoring or preaching that they are mistaken and misguided."[3]

Grady writes that after he published a previous book, *Ten Lies the Church Tells Women*, in 2000, his critics called him "Christian feminist," "egalitarian," "liberal," and "heretic."[4]

Another survey respondent suggested women read Wayne Grudem's and John Piper's book, *Recovering Biblical Manhood and Womanhood*.

A Texas woman told me to read 1 Timothy 3:12, and wrote: "Only men should be deacons." Yet an Oklahoma woman reminded me that Phoebe was a "deaconess" (Romans 16:1).

A woman from Georgia told me that Paul said: "Women are not to speak in church" (quoting 1 Corinthians 14:34–35: "Women should remain silent in the churches. They are not allowed to speak, but must be in submission.... It is disgraceful for a woman to speak in the church"). Yet another reminded me that Paul actually gives instructions to women when they pray or prophesy in worship: "And every woman who prays or prophesies with her head uncovered dishonors her head" (1 Corinthians 11:5).

Another quoted 1 Timothy 2:12: "I do not allow a woman to teach or exercise authority over a man" (NASB), and told me that women aren't supposed to teach or be in authority over men. Yet another reminded me that first-century Christian women did, indeed, "teach" and "exercise authority" over men (referring to Priscilla in Acts 18:26).

(handwritten margin note: In what context.)

I heard from both sides—those who follow a literal interpretation of Scripture and believe women should work in subordinate church roles, and those who quoted Galatians 3:27–28 and told me women, like men, should be church leaders.

THE SUBMISSIVE VIEW OF WOMEN

The following responses support the view that women in the church should have a submissive role:

From Alabama: "Many times churches overlook skills that women possess that can enhance and enrich leadership in the church. Women shouldn't be the majority of leadership in the church, however, but they do add value to the church."

From Texas: "I believe women have lost the original role God gave them: to support their husbands and raise their children."

From Virginia: "I am a strong supporter of male headship—however, it would be wise on any pastor's part to address the often biased view of women in leadership. While I am not advocating equality in terms of positions/office within the church, I do believe the average pastor is unaware of the internal struggles that women deal with when they are 'called to ministry.' Most women are afraid they will be misunderstood if they seek to live out their call. I still feel the sting of embarrassment when my aunt rebuked me publicly and told me women could not preach. She said, 'You can be a missionary, but not a preacher!' I felt humiliated. Didn't God say that 'in the last days he would pour out his Spirit on *all* flesh—that both *sons and daughters* would prophesy'?"

From Nebraska: "The women in my church don't want to hold leadership positions! They are grateful they are quietly overlooked."

From Alabama: "I appreciate my pastor's recognition that women are also gifted by the Holy Spirit, and by his willingness to allow women to use those gifts in the church body. Finding the balance of women in leadership, without usurping the roles men should play, is key."

From Oregon: "Pastor, women are capable, dedicated, and spiritually equipped to do most any task needed in the church. Women are ready, willing, and able to help the church in the Great Commission, and to further God's kingdom here on earth. However, I'm not one of those women who *have* to be deacons or committee chairpersons to be recognized as a leader. Women have their own niche to fill in the church, and I'm perfectly happy to be used where I'm most needed."

From Florida: "Pastor, women are as capable as men to serve in church leadership roles, but we women don't want to take over the church leadership unless the men refuse to take the lead."

THE EGALITARIAN VIEW

I was overwhelmed by the sheer number of women—from a vast number of denominations—who sided with the egalitarian view—and believed women should be given the opportunity to serve in "male-dominated" (their word) church leadership positions. Pastor, be forewarned—you may find some of these responses offensive, hostile, and angry. With the clear understanding that I am "reporting," and not necessarily offering my personal opinion, I share some of their statements:

From Oklahoma: "When I was growing up in Baptist churches, with a background of three generations of Baptists, I remember women being asked by the local church to serve in leadership capacities. The church and individuals believed the Lord led them—and so do I. My firm belief is the Holy Spirit calls women to fill all positions of religious life. Women of the Bible were leaders through the ages, and prophets predicted it would continue. Women have been excluded from church leadership in the last several years. I think this is because of teachings and remarks made by pastors and denominational leaders."

From Georgia: "I can serve and I can do. I have talents I am unable to use in the church because I am a woman. I have organizational and management skills I use every day in the secular world, but I am not allowed to use my skills in the church—because I am a woman. Therefore, I am deprived of service."

From Washington state: "Women are as capable as men to hold leadership positions in the church. In many denominations, women are not regarded as eligible to hold certain positions. They are treated as second-class citizens."

From North Carolina: "Pastor, 60 percent of the church's resources are not used when women are not allowed to serve in the church! I believe God

Since when does God's will (or casting) to the Bible?

calls us all to do whatever needs to be done, and it is absolutely wrong for anyone to stand in the way of his will!"

From Alabama: "Male-dominated church leaders do not accept the fact that women are capable of holding leadership roles in church! The reason? Because of tradition and 'we have always done it this way.'"

From Illinois: "Women are very spiritual, they study, and they can lead the congregation very well. Many women are held back by preachers who do not think women should lead a congregation. We need more women in church leadership!"

From New York: "Women in [my denomination] for the most part are overlooked—especially as worship leaders. I find it particularly offensive that women rarely pray and/or even read Scripture from the platform. I am grieved every year at deacon nomination when all the men of the church—whether they are active or inactive members—are eligible to be deacons, yet women are not even considered."

From North Carolina: "Pastor, you should consider women for positions of leadership with the same consideration you afford men!"

From California: "Women can do other things besides cook and greet! Women should be used in ministry to reach out to all kinds of people. I don't mean cooking and greeting are not an important part of the church's ministry. But I think a lot of women in church can contribute more to church ministry. We have a lack of women leaders in our church."

From Iowa: "Most congregations in my denomination are led predominantly by male leaders. But I believe it is important to have both men and women represented in church leadership. I'd like to see a pastorally gifted woman on our staff. I'm not advocating an all-female staff, but I believe both genders should serve in leadership. I see an overreaction to women in ministry. On one hand, churches bar women from taking leadership positions. On the other, I see women who are 'unbecoming' in trying to act like a man in their leadership styles. I pray for the day when men and women will be in communion with one another and both serving the body of Christ in leadership roles."

From Tennessee: "Pastor, leadership and headship aren't always the same. Women are capable and viable leaders in many leadership arenas without usurping the headship role of a man."

From New England: "Women have the capability to serve in positions other than the decoration, kitchen, and nursery committees! I am blessed with a pastor who recognizes that women can bring wisdom, discernment, and knowledge to positions historically held only by men."

From South Dakota: "Women can and need to be allowed to pray in public worship services! Why is it that in my church only men are called on to pray in worship services? Is it because women's voices are soft and cannot be heard in a large sanctuary? The whole church misses out when we don't allow women to publicly pray."

From Minnesota: "Women are important! Important in the church as deacons too!"

From Pennsylvania: "Pastors need to acknowledge the fact that many women are just as capable as men to serve in leadership positions in church—such as moderator, deacon, and most certainly in leading coeducational spiritual formation groups. In my experience, women make better deacons (serving as family ministers) because: they usually have more discretionary time; they are often already doing the ministering tasks as church members; many of them have better skills than men for helping those in need. As for being qualified as a moderator, many women have experience in workplace management, and also have the personal skills needed for this kind of leadership. I don't know many laymen who are leading spiritual formation groups, but I do know several women who have organized and promoted these groups."

From Alabama: "Galatians 3:28 should guide the ministry of a pastor! What a huge mistake is the present denominational 'mantra' to dictate whom God calls for what task. It is God who gifts Christians and calls both male and female. We don't need pastors who set themselves up to 'play God' for us."

From Nebraska: "In most churches, women are not allowed to serve in their spiritual giftedness. What if God chooses to gift a woman with the gift of administration, prophecy, teaching, pastoring, and exhortation? These gifts in a man would certainly lead to ordination, and he would be empowered to lead a church. But what about these gifts given to a woman? Pastor, the message of the kingdom suffers because women are not empowered to serve God in the ways he has called them and equipped them."

From Oklahoma: "A woman can pray meaningfully before the congregation or read Scripture passages as well as any male deacon, pastor, or director of missions. A woman can be a worthy confidant, keeping facts about church business and personal information as skillfully as an FBI agent."

From Georgia: "Times are changing, and we're beginning to see more women in positions of church leadership. It's empowering to see women take leadership roles in church. It shows the world that God can use women in the work of his kingdom just as he uses them to minister in everyday life."

From Maine: "Pastors are apt to be too chauvinistic and do not always respect or accept women pastors. I've met quite a few women who were very good in the pulpit! Women are more qualified than men in a lot of areas of church leadership!"

From Tennessee: "Women are able to do other things besides teach young children or prepare fellowship meals. God has called women to minister! His 'anointing' shall be poured out upon sons *and* daughters. And, as *daughters*, we have a place in ministry leadership."

From Canada: "Romans 7 says we all are gifted by God for ministry. What about women who have the gift of leadership? Is this gift relegated only to Sunday school or women's ministry? If so, the entire church may end up being the loser. Women do bring a different perspective, and without that input, again, it seems to me, the church is the loser. There is a level of frustration among Christian women because there is a lack of opportunity to serve in leadership roles ... as compared to kitchen duties. There is an underlying frustration with women whose ministry gifts are in leadership. As a result, some are serving in the community, outside the church, which in fact may be the way the Lord gets other things done, apart from the local congregation."

From Maryland: "I went to seminary! So let me do the same things the 'preacher boys' do—lead a worship service, preach occasionally, etc. The problem is that too many men have outdated notions regarding a 'woman's place' in church, and these notions are based more on culture and tradition than on the Bible."

From Arizona: "Jesus understood men and women on a one-on-one basis—gender was irrelevant. If that was and is true, then women should be looked upon as equals among men. Qualified women should be allowed to hold, or perform, any job in the church that qualified men are allowed to do. Gender should not enter into the process of qualification."

From Tennessee: "Women can serve in vital roles in the local church. Since so many of today's church women have leadership roles in the workplace, these talents and abilities need to be utilized in the local church as well. So often women are asked to serve in service roles, such as Sunday school teachers, children's choir workers, or on aesthetics committees, but often times their gifts are in leadership. Women can serve as church leaders, and should be allowed to."

JUST PLAIN CONFUSED

I also heard from a number of Christian women who told me they were "just plain confused" about the interpretation of God's Word when the Bible speaks about women's roles in the church.

"I do not have a clear picture of what God approves on these issues. So many references to Scripture have been tossed around, taken out of context, and dissected to the point that I am confused. In my church, we *daily* battle denominational doctrine and legalistic issues, and it hinders the growth and unification of the whole body. I simply want to serve Christ—that's all." (Louisiana)

"I have a question: Is [the idea] that all the leadership is male, and women cannot take part in leadership roles, due to the man being the one who is 'over' the woman? I don't understand." (Tennessee)

DISCUSS GENDER LEADERSHIP VIEWS IN THE CHURCH

Many women write about the need to talk about different gender leadership views in the church, discuss the Scripture passages that are confusing to members, and openly dialogue the issues between men and women in the congregation.

The comments of an Alabama woman sum it up well:

I have always felt supported by the pastoral staff in the churches where we have been members. I am involved in a denomination that takes a conservative view of women in the church. I think a lot of times, men are unsure about what to do with women who have gifts in the areas of teaching and leadership. I would appreciate open dialogue about women's roles, knowing what the expectations are for women in the church, and knowing where the men believe women should be limited in their leadership roles. I would like the pastor to know I have questions about what my biblical role is as a woman leader in the church. Sometimes nothing is said until a "perceived line" is crossed, and then misunderstandings and alienation occur between the male leadership and the woman who has "crossed the line." Pastors need a woman's perspective on more than just hospitality, mercy, and children's ministries. Spiritual women in the church should be consulted on areas of ministry development and church discipline issues. Women who are capable in other vocational areas could be helpful by offering counsel on matters in the church. I believe women could be utilized more in the leadership of the church without compromising biblical roles of authority, much as a husband and wife cooperate and encourage each other's giftedness in a healthy marriage.

"We may never resolve all our differences about women in leadership," writes Terry Muck. "But we can help each other toward better understanding."[5]

SURVEY SUMMARY

Today's Christian woman wants her pastor to know that:

- Christian women are divided in their opinions on a woman's role in church leadership. Some think women should not be serving in church leadership positions because Scripture forbids it. But the majority believe women should be serving in all areas of church leadership, and not forbidden from any leadership position.
- A number of Christian women are confused about how to correctly interpret the Scriptures that speak to the issue of women in church leadership.
- Many women feel the need to talk about the different gender leadership views in the church, to discuss what the Scripture passages say, and to openly dialogue the issues with men and women in the congregation.

CHAPTER 14

"PASTOR, PLEASE PUT ME TO WORK"

*Many women, including myself, are struggling to find
where we fit into the church in regard to how God wants
us to use our spiritual gifts. I know who I am in Christ,
and I know what God has called me—and gifted me—to
do. However, I feel inhibited and underutilized. I have
a heart for Christ, and the desire to serve him as he has
called me to do. But where in the church? And where do
I start? Christ has gifted all of us, men and women. I am
eager to serve in some specific ministry capacity.*

A survey respondent from Texas

MANY YEARS AGO, I WORKED with the pastors and staff of the
Old South Church in downtown Boston, Massachusetts. A historic
church—and still thriving today—Old South was one of America's
earliest congregations, established in 1669. In 1875, members con-
structed a new church building in Boston's Back Bay area, and moved
the congregation from its former location on Washington Street.

Throughout its many years, the church has discovered some forgotten,
hidden treasures within its walls. In an old iron safe on the building's third
floor, church staff discovered Benjamin Franklin's original 1706 baptismal
certificate. Franklin's family, active members of Old South Church, had
lived across the street.

During the Revolutionary War, Old South Church pastor Thomas
Prince hid his vast library of rare books in the church's attic. Although
the British burned many of the books for firewood, Prince donated the

surviving volumes to the church. Later, discovered within that remaining collection were two copies of the 1640 *Bay Psalm Book*, the first book entirely written and printed in the new colonies. In the 1970s, Sothebys estimated the books' values to be $5 million and $8 million!

And that's not all! During the 1970s and '80s, when the congregation renovated Old South's century-old building, they found more hidden, valuable, and forgotten treasures. Beneath the pale gray paint (applied to the worship center's walls in 1950) lay an artist's lovely and original 1875 hand-stenciled patterns. And when workers removed the sanctuary's cupola cover, they discovered beautiful deep-purple glass, created in 1905 by Louis Comfort Tiffany himself!

Valuable, hidden, and newly discovered treasure found within the walls of Boston's Old South Church! What's my point?

YOUR CHURCH'S HIDDEN TREASURES

Pastor, you also have "treasures" hidden within the walls of your church! You have "living treasures" far more valuable than yellowed baptism certificates, Bay Psalm books, and Tiffany glass! I guarantee you, if you'll tap into these treasures, you will discover a richness and vitality that will renew and energize your congregation's ministry both inside and outside the church's walls!

What is this undiscovered treasure? Your church's Christian women! They tell me they are willing and eager to work hard for you and your congregation; they want to use their spiritual gifts in God's work through your ministry; and they are "sitting on the edges of their pews" waiting for you to direct and guide them. How can you harness the collective physical and spiritual energy of your church's women, and put them to work in your church? In this chapter I'll briefly share six suggestions.

1. SHARE YOUR CHURCH VISION

Share your vision for the church with your Christian women. Every church needs a vision—a ministry map that guides the congregation to attempt to do great things for God. The wise pastor writes down the vision—clearly and concisely—and keeps it always in front of the congregation. He then expects all ministry done by the church to aim toward fulfilling that vision, that goal. Women, like men, are goal-driven. They want to accomplish something of eternal significance—something that will last into the future. They want to leave a legacy. They don't work with the same heartfelt diligence when the goal is fuzzy or abstract.

Keep them informed of the church's plans. Show them the importance of their involvement. Supply them with the materials they need. And then watch them "catch fire"! They want to make a difference in the church, community, and world for Christ.

"If our vision and purpose is vague," writes a Florida woman, "we may be busy in church and even self-sacrifice, but we can't adequately harness our spiritual gifts for the glory of God."

You might also want to bring your church's women together to pray for your church and its ministry. Most Christian women place great value on their personal prayer life. In fact, many are prayer warriors! Give them something specific to pray about, and watch what happens!

2. VALUE WOMEN'S INSIGHTS

Value women's insights, take seriously their input, and help them implement their ideas into the overall vision of the church.

A Texas woman writes: "I wish my pastor could show me how to use my creative ideas and spiritual gifts in a practical way to help accomplish the mission of the church. I need help to implement my gifts and 'release' my creativity."

A Michigan woman writes: "I wish my pastor understood the remarkable gifts of our church's women. He is missing opportunities that God has placed all around him. If our women were allowed to use their gifts in the church, the whole body would benefit greatly."

"Many of us women in the church are professionals in the outside business world," writes another. "We are educated with a variety of gifts the church could use. Please talk to us, find out what we do well, and then use us in the church."

3. PINPOINT A WOMAN'S GIFTS

Pinpoint each woman's individual spiritual gift(s) and equip her to use them for the benefit of the church. I heard complaints from numerous women who work in various church jobs, but often feel inadequate for those positions, or don't enjoy the work they are asked to do. Some dread getting up in the morning and fulfilling their assigned church duties.

Let me give you an example. My friend, Tara, a mother with grown children, loves babies. She thinks they are adorable. She looks forward with great eagerness to the day she has grandchildren. But Tara's spiritual gifts lie in the area of theology and teaching. While she has agreed, on many occasions, to work in the church nursery, she finds that the hours drag, and she dreams of teaching adult Sunday school women instead. You see, Tara is not spiritually gifted to work in the nursery, and she just can't get too excited about that area of ministry. She does it, but she doesn't enjoy it. Teaching adult Sunday school, however, is another story. She loves it! She spends hours each week studying Scripture and organizing her teaching notes. She jumps out of bed on Sunday mornings, and goes to church early to ready her Sunday school classroom and personally greet each member as she comes in the door.

On the other hand, Tara's friend, Charlene has no desire to teach adult women in Sunday school. But she possesses very capable spiritual gifts to work with the nursery's babies. She loves cuddling those babies and making sure their diapers are clean when parents pick them up. She moves from bed to bed, and from child to child, silently blessing and praying for each infant. When she's in the nursery on Sunday mornings, she complains that the hours pass by much too quickly.

Common human logic reveals a workable solution: Enlist the Taras of your church to teach Sunday school. Enlist the Charlenes to work in the nursery. It seems quite simple, but it's not being done that way in many churches. Too often the Taras are in the nurseries and the Charlenes are teaching Sunday school.

It's no wonder so many women are dissatisfied with their churches and frustrated in their individual ministries there. Women are given different gifts to use in God's service. Scripture states: "There are different kinds of gifts, but the same Spirit. There are different kinds of service, but the same Lord. There are different kinds of working, but the same God works all of them." Scripture also claims that each of the Spirit's different gifts is "given for the common good.... All these are the work of one and the same Spirit, and he gives them to each one, just as he determines." (See 1 Corinthians 12:4–11.)

Why do churches so often enlist and expect women to work in areas when they have no gifts to contribute to that particular position? While these jobs may be essential to the life of the church, they are so much better accomplished by a woman who is gifted in those areas. We must take the time, energy, and forethought to match the gifts of women with the jobs we ask them to do!

One woman writes: "Pastor, please let us serve according to the Spirit's giftings rather than according to cultural or church expectations."

Another writes: "My desire as a woman is to serve under my pastor's leadership using my calling and giftedness."

"A pastor should learn each woman's individual spiritual gifts," writes another, "and help her find a place in the church to use them."

Many women expressed this same wish. "I wish more pastors would encourage women to use their spiritual gifts in the church."

"Pastor, please make good use of the gifts God has given the women in your church!"

"We want opportunities to use our God-given gifts in the church. Please help us find ways to focus and use our creativity."

Another woman reminded me: "The same Holy Spirit who gifts my pastor, and the men in my church, also gifts me and the church's women! We're all members of the body. We're all needed in ministry!"

One particular letter from an Alabama grandmother touched my heart. "I am singlehandedly raising my mentally retarded and physically challenged eleven-year-old grandson full-time. I also work full-time at an hourly wage job. I can't always make it to church during the week, but I always make sure we attend worship services on Sunday mornings. I can't do much, but I'm a good reader. I'd love to be the person who reads the church's prayer list on Sunday mornings during the worship service. My pastor sometimes has trouble pronouncing the names, and I feel like that's something I could do. I'd be able to participate more actively in church, and at the same time, take some pressure off my pastor. I really do want to be involved in the ministry of my church."

4. EMPOWER THE WOMEN IN YOUR CHURCH

Empower women with prayer, and invite them to plug in to the ongoing ministry of the church.

An Ohio woman writes: "Women want to be included in all aspects of the church. When their giftings and talents are affirmed and encouraged, women can and will contribute in a powerful manner. Empower a woman to do a job, and you will have a mighty force to deal with."

Another writes: "Help us find our calling to ministry, and then bless us and help us fulfill our ministries. We've let the world entice women to work their heads off in the secular world, but we are finding no fulfillment and satisfaction because we want to use that energy for church ministry."

"I'd like to see my pastor harness the spiritual gifts of the women in the church," writes an Oklahoma woman, "and use those gifts to enrich the congregation, community, and the world! Please don't box us in—let us freely use our gifts!"

Another writes: "Pastor, encourage your church's women to pursue their gifts and use them in the church. Allow them to use their hearts and their talents to reach unique, specific people groups in their communities. Help women to think through and articulate their gifts and callings. I know of so many women in the church who are 'chomping at the bit' to use their giftedness and talents, but who feel they can't, or that they can't find the right avenue."

As you enlist women to plug into the church's ministries, be sure to provide them with the necessary help they need. Women work well in pairs and on teams. When they work alone, they can quickly feel isolated, overwhelmed, and too pressured to get it all done. Be careful not to overload women with too much work. They can easily become so "stretched out," they can't do any of the jobs well.

5. EQUIP WOMEN TO LAUNCH NEW MINISTRIES

Women crave the opportunities to help launch new ministries in the church. They long for their pastor to hear their ideas for new programs that will reach out and provide ministry to others. Women are great brainstormers, as well as accomplished problem solvers. Give them the chance to show you what they can do. Equip them and empower them to move ahead in ministry.

As I write these words, however, I can empathize with the church pastor who truly wants to empower and equip the church's women to discover new ways to minister, and to lead the church in new programs, but encounters resistance from others. The "others" may be members of a conservative church board, or long-standing deacons, or elders in the church. The "others" may be church members — both men and women — who resist change, new programs, and even fresh church growth. In such situations, the pastor may need to "educate" his congregation, and be careful to take slowly the amount of change he brings into the church. In some churches, only over time does the pastor see positive change happen. But the important thing is that it may actually happen one day.

A Mississippi mom writes: "Pastor, I need you to 'authorize' me to use my spiritual gift in a specific task. Don't ask me to 'just do something.' Actually 'authorize' me to do it. Then make sure I have the resources and authority necessary to accomplish the task. When you ask me to contribute my gifts to the ministry of the church, but give me no recognized authority to make the task happen, I get frustrated."

Another writes from Indiana: "Give me a responsibility, and let me show you I am fully capable of doing it. Make sure you give me what I need to do the job, and empower me to get it done. Help me with budget needs, as well as policies I need to know, contacts I need to make, etc."

"Pastor," a Michigan woman writes, "most Christian women want to be used by the church. Most of us have some great ideas for new ministries that would reach out and touch the congregation and community around us. Give us a chance to tell you about these ideas, and then help us get them going!"

6. ALL GOD'S WORK IS VALUABLE

Assure the women in your church that whatever the Spirit has called and gifted them to do, their work is valuable to the ministry and vision of the church. Every job done by women in the church—as long as it is endowed with the Spirit's gifting and calling—is tremendously important to God and the church body. We often hear about women in the Bible who held important positions and did great things for God. Women like Deborah, Israel's great patriotic leader; Esther, the Israelites' defender and deliverer; Mary, the woman chosen by God to give birth to the Christ child; and Lydia, the successful business woman from Thyatira who so ably ministered to Paul when he visited Philippi.

But Scripture also shows us other women who played much smaller roles in ministry, whose work proved just as necessary and important.

Consider the influence and impact of Dorcas (Tabitha), who served God as a simple but benevolent seamstress. Dorcas unselfishly sewed clothes for her city's impoverished widows (Acts 9:36–42).

Consider Abigail, wife of the "surly and mean" Nabal—"a wicked man that no one can talk to" (1 Samuel 25:3, 17). She used her simple gifts of good judgment and kindness to welcome and feed David and his men. In doing so, she saved the sorry life of her husband, "Fool" (see v. 25). And David rewarded her: "Praise be to the LORD, the God of Israel, who has sent you today to meet me. May you be blessed for your good judgment and for keeping me from bloodshed this day and from avenging myself with my own hands.... If you had not come quickly to meet me, not one male belonging to Nabal would have been left alive by daybreak" (vv. 32–34).

Consider the Shunammite, a hospitable woman who offered a little rooftop room, a table, a chair, and a lamp for the prophet Elisha. So touched was Elisha by her simple generosity, he asked God to give her a son. And when her son mysteriously died, Elisha prayed to God, who brought the child back to life (2 Kings 4:8–37).

No woman's God-given gift is too simple to be used for the glory of God. As her pastor, you can help her focus her gift so that her work—no matter how small or seemingly insignificant—can produce a tremendous harvest for God. Consider Mother Teresa's ministry to the poor of India. She felt that her God-given gift of compassion was a small and simple gift. Yet God used this gentle woman to influence a world.

"We ourselves feel that what we are doing is just a drop in the ocean," Mother Teresa acknowledged. "But if that drop was not in the ocean, I think the ocean will be less because of that missing drop."[1]

And, indeed, the ocean and the church would surely be less without Mother Teresa's gifts and work. God intends that all women in the congregation contribute to the church's ministry with the gifts that he himself has endowed them.

OTHER BENEFITS TO THE CHURCH

When pastors encourage women to use their God-given spiritual gifts in the church, they see other benefits besides the obvious ones. For instance, a woman who is happy and content in the church usually involves her husband and children in church. When women are encouraged, equipped, and empowered to embrace their individual ministries in the church, and find joy and fulfillment, they most often invite their friends to visit, join, and participate in the ministry of the church. Other members of the church often "catch" a woman's enthusiasm in her church work, and they join in and help her accomplish the church's vision. The entire congregation—and often the community—benefits from the results of a woman's ministry to them. Christian women, working in their gifted areas, have changed the face of many churches, communities, and nations.

Pastor, also know that when you pinpoint women's gifts, and equip, enable, empower, and expect them to use their gifts for the benefit of the congregation and community, you will produce faithful and fulfilled women who will most likely stay active in their church's steadily growing and thriving ministries.

"The church will last for eternity," writes Rick Warren, "and because it is God's instrument for ministry here on earth, it is truly the *greatest force on the face of the planet*.... God will give us his power to complete the task. This is God's way—ordinary people empowered by his Spirit."[2]

An Indiana woman writes: "If a job needs to be done in the church, know that women are the best ones to get things done!"

Expect great things from the women in your church, for they are truly your church's "hidden treasure"! I can guarantee you they will live up to your challenge, bless others, and bring blessings to your entire congregation!

Today's Christian woman wants her pastor to:

- Know she is gifted by God for ministry.
- Share with her the church's vision.
- Value her insights, take seriously her input, and help her implement her ideas into the overall vision of the church.
- Pinpoint her individual spiritual gift(s), and equip her to use her spiritual gift(s) for the benefit of the church.
- Empower her with prayer, and invite her to plug into the ongoing ministry of the church.
- Appreciate her God-given gifts and abilities no matter how small they may be.
- Brainstorm potential new ministry possibilities with her, and then equip and empower her to launch them.
- Support her with your prayers, and supply her ministry's needs.
- Encourage her in God's work and expect great things from her!

NOTES

INTRODUCTION

1. Rick Warren, "Instrument of Blessing," *The Alabama Baptist*, January 19, 2006, 19.

2. Thom S. Rainer, *High Expectations: The Remarkable Secret for Keeping People in Your Church* (Nashville: Broadman and Holman, 1999), 1.

3. *www.barna.org/FlexPage.aspx?Page=Topic&TopicID=14* (accessed January 19, 2006).

4. In 1950, no one had heard of Goddess spirituality; now ... the Goddess is being proclaimed and celebrated in important sectors of modern society, and she shows no sign of retreating to her previous state of obscurity.... The Goddess movement makes provocative assertions in fields as diverse as theology, anthropology, ancient history, sociology, psychology, and art history. Goddess spirituality is alive and well and gaining credibility on our nation's university campuses. Some universities are offering classes on witchcraft and magic as part of their curriculum, and sponsoring Pagan Society clubs for their students. From: *www.boundless.org/2002_2003/features/a0000712.html* (accessed January 18, 2006); *www.boundless.org/1999/departments/pages/a0000032.html* (accessed January 18, 2006).

5. *www.barna.org/FlexPage.aspx?Page=BarnaUpdatenarrow&BarnaUpdateID=216* (accessed January 24, 2006).

6. Charles Swindoll, *Simple Faith* (Dallas: Word, 1991), 118.

7. George Barna, *www.barna.org/FlexPage.aspx?Page=Excerpt&ProductID=55* (accessed June 15, 2005).

8. The Barna Group, "Women Are the Backbone of the Christian Congregations in America," March 6, 2000, *www.barna.org/FlexPage.aspx?Page=BarnaUpdate&BarnaUpdateID=47* (accessed June 28, 2005).

9. Warren, "Instrument of Blessing," 19 (emphasis mine).

CHAPTER 1: "PASTOR, I'M TIRED"

1. John Eldredge, *Wild at Heart* (Nashville: Thomas Nelson, 2001), 17.

2. George Barna, *www.barna.org/FlexPage.aspx?Page=BarnaUpdate&BarnaUpdateID=47* (accessed June 28, 2005; emphasis mine).

3. See Proverbs 31:13, 15, 17, 18, 27, 29.

4. Charles R. Swindoll, *Stress Fractures* (Portland, Ore.: Multnomah, 1990), 155.

5. Diane Passno, *Feminism: Mystique or Mistake?* (Wheaton, Ill.: Tyndale, 2000), 118.

6. Thomas à Kempis, in Richard J. Foster and Emilie Griffin, *Spiritual Classics* (San Francisco: HarperSanFrancisco, 2000), 149.

7. See my Bible study for women, *Come to the Quiet: The Secrets of Solitude and Rest* (Minneapolis: Bethany House, 2003).

8. Betty Cuniberti, "Are Working Mothers Really Pioneers?" *The Courier-Journal* (Louisville, Ky.), August 16, 1987, H6.

9. Stacy Wiebe, "Tips for Women Who Juggle Too Much," *www.womentoday magazine.com/career/busyness.html* (accessed July 15, 2005).

10. Henri J. M. Nouwen, *Making All Things New* (New York: Phoenix Press, Walker and Company, 1981), 23.

11. Swindoll, *Simple Faith* (Dallas: Word, 1991), 222.

CHAPTER 2: "PASTOR, I HURT"

1. Arthur Gish, *Beyond the Rat Race* (Scottdale, Pa.: Herald Press, 1973), 20.

2. Ruth Haley Barton, "Are You Dangerously Tired?" *www.christianitytoday.com/ childrensministry/articles/le_040408.html* (accessed July 30, 2005).

3. Karl Menninger, *Whatever Became of Sin?* (New York: Hawthorn Books, 1973), 91.

4. Ibid.

5. John Michael Talbot with Steve Rabey, *The Lessons of St. Francis* (New York: Penguin, 1997), 21.

6. Paul Brand and Philip Yancey, *In His Image* (Grand Rapids, Mich.: Zondervan, 1984), 255.

7. Susan Forward, *Emotional Blackmail* (New York: HarperCollins, 1997), 135.

8. American Society of Reproductive Medicine, U.S. 1997, *www.wrongdiagnosis.com/ i/infertility/stats.htm* (accessed January 27, 2006). "Treatment for Infertility Is a Thriving $1 Billion Per Year Industry!" *www.yourfuturehealth.com/resources_statistics.htm#infertility* (accessed January 27, 2006).

9. Peri Stone-Palmquist, "Suicide: A Preventable Tragedy," *Christianity Today*, June 12, 2000; *www.christianitytoday.com/global/printer.html?/ct/2000/007/8.74.html* (accessed January 28, 2006).

10. *www.agi-usa.org/pubs/fb_teen_sex.html* (accessed January 27, 2006).

11. Professor David Fergusson, director of the Christchurch Health and Development Study in New Zealand, and two colleagues, L. John Horwood and Elizabeth Ridder, conducted a study on abortion and mental health. Their report states, "Those having an abortion [under age 25] had elevated rates of subsequent mental health problems including depression, anxiety, suicidal behaviours and substance use disorders." Their report goes on to say, "The findings suggest that abortion in young women may be associated with increased risks of mental health problems." ["The Elephant in the Living Room: The New Zealand Abortion Study," *Breakpoint*, February 24, 2006, *www.breakpoint.org* (accessed February 24, 2006).]

12. Post-abortion syndrome is a term used to describe the emotional and psychological consequences of abortion. They might include guilt, anger, anxiety (accompanied by tension, irritability, dizziness, upset stomach, headache, worry, and disturbed sleep, etc.), depression, a sense of loss, even thoughts of suicide. Feelings of rejection, low self-esteem, guilt and depression are all ingredients for suicide. According to one study, women who have had an abortion are nine times more likely to attempt suicide than women who have not. [*www. leaderu.com/orgs/tul/pap1.html* (accessed January 27, 2006).] The United States has one of the highest abortion rates among developed countries. Only 1 percent (or about 13,000) of the one million abortions that take place annually in the United States (equaling more than 43 million abortions in the US since 1973) will be attributed to rape and/or incest. [*www.family. org/cforum/fosi/bioethics/facts/a0027730.cfm* (accessed January 27, 2006).] Those most likely to have an abortion are women younger than twenty-five years old (52 percent), who are unmarried (51 percent), and already have one or more children (60 percent). Most abortions occur

during the first six to twelve weeks of pregnancy. [*womensissues.about.com/cs/abortionstats/a/ aaabortionstats.htm* (accessed January 27, 2006).]

13. Charles Colson, *Answers to Your Kids' Questions* (Wheaton, Ill.: Tyndale, 2000), 144.

14. *www.usnews.com/usnews/health/brain/alzheimers/alz.about.htm* (accessed January 27, 2006). That will certainly change the face of your congregation!

15. *www.mayoclinicproceedings.com/inside.asp?AID=402&UID=* (accessed January 27, 2006).

16. To help those like Elaine in your congregation, please see my book *Planting Trust, Knowing Peace* (Zondervan, 2005).

17. "In 1998 the prestigious American Journal of Preventative Medicine published a landmark study by a team of researchers at Kaiser Permanente Medical Care Program working with epidemiologists from the Centers for Disease Control (CDC) in Atlanta. The survey of nearly 20,000 people found that those with 'adverse childhood experiences' were, as adults, far more likely to suffer from cancer, heart disease, chronic lung disorders, and other leading causes of death.... Those who had encountered abuse (physical, psychological, or sexual), or were raised in dysfunctional families (with violence, substance abuse, mental illness, or criminal behavior), were far more likely to develop life-threatening illnesses. In fact, an adverse childhood proves to be as powerful a predictor of subsequent illness as smoking.... People whose early years are marked by emotional injury are far more likely to have high health risk factors. The study found a strong correlation between childhood adversity and obesity, physical inactivity, and smoking, as well as depression and suicide attempts." [Harold Bloomfield with Philip Goldberg, *Making Peace with Your Past* (New York: HarperCollins, 2000), preface.]

18. "Child Sexual Abuse," The American Academy for Child & Adolescent Psychiatry, July 2004, *www.aacap.org/publications/factsfam/sexabuse.htm* (accessed January 30, 2006).

19. "Child sexual abuse has been reported up to 80,000 times a year, but the number of unreported instances is far greater. Sexual abuse is painful and confusing to a child of five or older. When she knows and trusts the abuser, she becomes trapped between affection or loyalty for him, and the knowledge that the sexual activities are terribly wrong. If the child tries to break away from the abuse, the abuser may threaten her with violence or loss of love. When a child suffers prolonged sexual abuse, she may develop low self-esteem as an adult, a feeling of worthlessness, a distorted view of sex, and become withdrawn and mistrustful of people." ["Child Sexual Abuse," The American Academy for Child & Adolescent Psychiatry, July 2004, *www.aacap.org/publications/factsfam/sexabuse.htm* (accessed January 30, 2006).]

20. Jackie J. Hudson, "Characteristics of the Incestuous Family," in *Women, Abuse, and the Bible*, Catherine Clark Kroeger and James R. Beck, eds. (Grand Rapids, Mich.: Baker, 1996), 71.

21. Child sexual abuse is defined as "any sexual act with a child performed by an adult or an older child. This might be fondling the child's genitals; getting the child to fondle an adult's genitals; mouth to genital contact; rubbing an adult's genitals on the child; or actually penetrating the child's vagina or anus. Other forms of abuse can also occur that are not as easy to detect. These include showing an adult's genitals to a child, showing the child pornographic or 'dirty' pictures or videotapes, or using the child as a model to make pornographic materials. Boys and girls are abused in this way most often by adults or older children who are known to them and who can exert power over them. The victim knows the offender in 8 out of 10 reported cases. The offender is often an authority figure whom the

child trusts or loves. The offender persuades, bribes, tricks, or coerces the child to engage in sex or sexual acts." ["What Is Child Abuse?" The American Academy of Pediatrics, *www.medem.com/MedLB/article_detaillb.cfm?article_ID=ZZZ1LW3YA7C&sub_cat=348* (accessed January 30, 2006).]

22. Wm. J. Diehm, "How to Cope with Being Widowed," *http://seniors-site.com/widowm/coping.html* (accessed January 29, 2006).

23. Researchers admit that "women widowed less than a year reported more mental and physical problems than women ... who had been widowed for longer than a year. But the recently widowed women did improve over time and finding social support may be important in the coping process." [Sara Wilcox, "First Year of Widowhood Most Harmful to Mental Health—According to a Sample of Over 70,000 Middle Aged Women," The American Psychological Association (APA), *www.apa.org/releases/widowhood.html* (accessed January 29, 2006).]

24. For information about how you and your church can reach out to hurting women, see my book *God's Heart, God's Hands* (Birmingham, Ala.: New Hope, 1998).

CHAPTER 3: "PASTOR, I NEED BIBLICAL COUNSELING"

1. Harold Bloomfield with Philip Goldberg, *Making Peace with Your Past* (New York: HarperCollins, 2000), xiv.

2. Beverly White Hislop, *Shepherding a Woman's Heart* (Chicago: Moody Press, 2003), 29.

3. John Burke, *No Perfect People Allowed* (Grand Rapids, Mich.: Zondervan, 2005), 44.

4. John Gray, *Men Are from Mars, Women Are from Venus* (New York: HarperCollins, 1992), 10.

5. Ibid., 11.

6. Bill and Pam Farrel, *Men Are Like Waffles, Women Are Like Spaghetti* (Eugene, Ore.: Harvest House, 2001), 48.

7. Rob Jackson, "Who Needs It? The Importance of Counseling," Pure Intimacy, October 9, 2005, *www.pureintimacy.org/print_friendly.cfm?articleurl=/gr/intimacy/redemption/a0000* (accessed January 31, 2006).

8. Ibid.

9. Carolyn Custis James, *When Life and Beliefs Collide* (Grand Rapids, Mich.: Zondervan, 2001), 146 (emphasis mine).

10. Henri J. M. Nouwen, *Can You Drink the Cup?* (Notre Dame, Ind.: Ave Maria Press, 1996), 57, 58.

11. The story of Elizabeth's suicide was excerpted from my book *God's Heart, God's Hands* (Birmingham, Ala.: New Hope, 1998), 112–118.

CHAPTER 4: "PASTOR, I YEARN FOR CHRISTIAN FRIENDS AND FELLOWSHIP"

1. John Burke, *No Perfect People Allowed* (Grand Rapids, Mich.: Zondervan, 2005), 46.

2. Ibid., 45.

3. Prevention.com, "Love Keeps You Healthy," *www.prevention.com/article/0,5778,s1-6-83-147-6376-1,00.html* (accessed February 13, 2006).

4. Melissa Healy, "Women Gain Benefits by Good Female Friendships," *Los Angeles Times*, May 28, 2005, 1B, 6B.

5. Vickie Kraft, *Women Mentoring Women* (Chicago: Moody Press, 1992), 28.

6. Fisher Humphreys, *I Have Called You Friends* (Birmingham, Ala.: New Hope, 2005), 33.

7. Thom S. Rainer, *High Expectations: The Remarkable Secret for Keeping People in Your Church* (Nashville: Broadman and Holman, 1999), 130.

8. Beverly White Hislop, *Shepherding a Woman's Heart* (Chicago: Moody Press, 2003), 30.

9. "The word 'grief' refers to our subjective feelings and emotions after the loss of a loved one (usually through death, but also after the dissolution of a relationship). We call the collective processes by which we resolve grief 'mourning.' Grieving is the emotional and physical response to a loss, the process of coming to terms with it and letting go. Grieving takes a long time, and it is hard work." [David E. Larson, M.D., editor-in-chief, *Mayo Clinic Family Health Book*, second ed. (New York: William Morrow, 1996), 1109.]

10. Thom S. Rainer, *Effective Evangelistic Churches* (Nashville: Broadman and Holman, 1996), 180.

CHAPTER 5: "PASTOR, I CRAVE BIBLE STUDY AND SPIRITUAL GROWTH"

1. Carolyn Custis James, *When Life and Beliefs Collide* (Grand Rapids, Mich.: Zondervan, 2001), 95.

2. John Michael Talbot with Steve Rabey, *The Lessons of St. Francis* (New York: Penguin, 1997), 1.

3. Charles Colson, *Answers to Your Kids' Questions* (Wheaton, Ill.: Tyndale, 2000), 17.

4. Ibid., 113.

5. Diane Passno, *Feminism: Mystique or Mistake?* (Wheaton, Ill.: Tyndale, 2000), 123, 125.

6. Carolyn Custis James, *Lost Women of the Bible* (Grand Rapids, Mich.: Zondervan, 2005), 199.

7. Meister Eckhard, in Richard J. Foster and Emilie Griffin, *Spiritual Classics* (San Francisco: HarperSanFrancisco, 2000), 206.

8. Custis James, *When Life and Beliefs Collide*, 40.

9. Brennan Manning, *Ruthless Trust* (San Francisco: HarperSanFrancisco, 2000), 78.

10. The Barna Group, *www.barna.org/FlexPage.aspx?Page=BarnaUpdate&Barna UpdateID=192* (accessed February 6, 2006).

11. Ibid.

CHAPTER 6: "PASTOR, I HAVE PROBLEMS IN MY MARRIAGE"

1. Tim Kimmel, *Powerful Personalities* (Colorado Springs: Focus on the Family, 1993), 23.

2. Prevention.com, "Love Keeps You Healthy," *www.prevention.com/article/0,5778,s1-6-83-147-6376-1,00.html* (accessed February 13, 2006).

3. Robert S. McGee, *Search for Significance* (Nashville: LifeWay Press, 1992), 14.

4. Focus Ministries, *www.focusministries1.org/domestic_violence.html*, (accessed March 1, 2006).

5. Carolyn Holderread Heggen, "Religious Beliefs and Abuse," in *Women, Abuse, and the Bible*, Catherine Clark Kroeger and James R. Beck, eds. (Grand Rapids, Mich.: Baker, 1996), 15.

6. "Deadly Submission?" *Discipleship Journal*, July/August 2001, 14.

7. Focus Ministries, *http://www.focusministries1.org/domestic_violence.html* (accessed March 1, 2006).

8. Denise George, *God's Heart, God's Hands* (Birmingham, Ala.: New Hope, 1998), 76.

9. Holderread Heggen in *Women, Abuse, and the Bible*, 17.

10. Frank A. Thomas, *They Like to Never Quit Praisin' God* (Cleveland: Pilgrim Press, 1997), 59–60.

11. Steven R. Fleming, "Competent Christian Intervention with Men Who Batter," in *Women, Abuse, and the Bible*, 181.

12. Karl Menninger, *Whatever Became of Sin?* (New York: Hawthorn Books, 1973), 168.

13. Dr. Mark Laaser, in Lauren Winner, "The Next Big Challenge for Clergy," *www.beliefnet.com/story/61/story_6116 html* (accessed October 9, 2005).

14. Jane Lampman, "Churches Confront an 'Elephant in the Pews,'" csmonitor.com, *www.csmonitor.com/2005/0825/p14s01-lire.htm* (accessed October 9, 2005).

15. "One in five people in the pews has looked at web porn. Broken down further, the survey (by Focus on the Family and Zogby International) shows that one in every three men has looked at a sex site, and close to half of men under 35." [Lauren Winner, "The Next Big Challenge for Clergy," *www.beliefnet.com/story/61/story_6116 html* (accessed October 9, 2005).]

16. Simon Sheh (a psychologist of evangelical faith from Edmonton, Alberta), in Jane Lampman, "Churches Confront an 'Elephant in the Pews,'" csmonitor.com, *www.csmonitor.com/2005/0825/p14s01-lire.htm* (accessed October 9, 2005).

17. Anonymous, "Emily's Story," Pure Intimacy, *www.pureintimacy.org/print_friendly.cfm?articleurl=/gr/intimacy/information/a0000* (accessed October 9, 2005).

18. Ryan Hosley and Steve Watters, "Dangers and Disappointments of Pornography," Pure Intimacy, *www.pureintimacy.org/print_friendly.cfm?articleurl=/gr/intimacy/understanding/a00* (accessed October 9, 2005).

19. Ibid.

20. Definition by Lawrence J. Hatterer, author of *Changing Homosexuality in the Male*, in Frank Worthen, "What Is Homosexuality?" Pure Intimacy, *www.pureintimacy.org/print_friendly.cfm?articleurl=/gr/homosexuality/a0000054.cfm* (accessed October 9, 2005).

21. Elizabeth Warren, in Brigitte Yuille, "The Emotional Toll of Bankruptcy," Bankrate.com, *www.bankrate.com/nltrack/news/bankruptcy/20060118a2.asp* (accessed February 20, 2006).

22. John W. Schoen, "Help, I Can't Stop Shopping," MSNBC, *www.msnbc.msn.com/id/11275503/page/2/* (accessed February 13, 2006).

23. Addison Wiggin, "Pathological Consumption: What We Now Know," *www.investorsinsight.com* (accessed February 21, 2006).

24. Louis Uchitelle, "Women Forced to Delay Retirement," *New York Times* online, June 26, 2001.

25. Ibid.

CHAPTER 7: "PASTOR, MY CHILDREN ARE IMPORTANT TO ME"

1. Dr. Timothy George, in Denise George, *Teach Your Children to Pray* (Fearn, Scotland: Christian Focus Publications, 2004), 23–24.

2. Alistair Begg, *The Hand of God* (Chicago: Moody Press, 1999), 24.

3. *www.barna.org/FlexPage.aspx?Page=BarnaUpdate&BarnaUpdateID=183* (accessed June 28, 2005).

4. *http://abcnews.go.com/GMA/print?id=488197*, posted February 18, 2005 (accessed March 7, 2005).

5. *www.focusonyourchild.com/hottopics/a0001050.cf*m (accessed March 7, 2006).

6. "The number of women employed outside the home continues to increase (as high as two-thirds of all U.S. adult women are employed, and three-fourths of all employed women are working full-time). More than six in ten women in the U.S. workforce have children younger than three. The number of female-headed households continues to rise." [Beverly White Hislop, *Shepherding a Woman's Heart* (Chicago: Moody Press, 2003), 79.]

7. Through local groups that provide a caring atmosphere, MOPS helps today's mother of young children (from infancy through kindergarten) establish and maintain helpful relationships. For information about MOPS, write to: Mothers of Preschoolers International, P.O. Box 102200, Denver, CO 80250-2200, or call: 303-733-5353; visit their website at *www.mops.org*; or email info@mops.org.

8. U.S. Census Bureau, *http://chhs.gsu.edu/nationalcenter/welcome.html* (accessed March 7, 2006).

9. *www.census.gov/population/www/documentation/twps0026/twps0026.html* (accessed March 7, 2006).

10. Ibid.

11. Ibid.

12. *http://chhs.gsu.edu/nationalcenter/welcome.html* (accessed March 7, 2006).

13. "The Private World of Bill Gates: A Surprising Visit with the Man Who Is Shaping Our Future," *Time*, January 13, 1997, 51.

14. David Murrow, *Why Men Hate Going to Church* (Nashville: Thomas Nelson, 2005), 5.

15. Ibid., 19.

16. Ibid., 79.

17. Joseph F. Girzone, *Never Alone* (New York: Doubleday, 1994), 11–12.

18. "Worst Directions," *Parade*, December 26, 2004, 6.

19. Elizabeth Achtemeier, *Not Til I Have Done* (Louisville, Ky.: Westminster/John Knox Press, 1999), 123.

20. Today's families are threatened and fragmented. Statistics tell us that only 34 percent of all children will live with both biological parents through age eighteen. [Focus on the Family, "The Breakdown of the Family," *www.focusonyourchild.com/develop/art1/A0000670.html* (accessed March 7, 2006).] A recent study, conducted by Ellison Research, among a representative sample of 695 Protestant church ministers nationwide, asked pastors to identify "the three strongest threats to families in their own community." Pastors listed, as the top three threats, "divorce (listed as one of the top three by 43 percent of all ministers), negative influences from the media (38 percent), and materialism (36 percent). These were followed by absentee fathers (24 percent) and families that lack a stay-at-home parent (22 percent)." ["Threats to the Family," Ellison Research, *www.ellisonresearch.com/ERPS%20II/release_13_family.htm* (accessed March 2, 2006).]

21. Charles Colson, *Answers to Your Kids' Questions* (Wheaton, Ill.: Tyndale, 2000), xxvii.

22. Alice P. Mathews, *Preaching That Speaks to Women* (Grand Rapids, Mich.: Baker Academic, 2003), 155.

23. *www.family.org/resources/itempg.cfm?itemid=1850* (accessed March 7, 2006).

24. Excerpted from Joshua Coleman, *The Lazy Husband: How to Get Your Men to Do More Parenting and Housework, http://abcnews.go.com/GMA/print?id=488197*, February 18, 2005 (accessed March 7, 2005).

CHAPTER 8: "PASTOR, WHEN YOU PREACH ..."

1. Alice P. Mathews, *Preaching That Speaks to Women* (Grand Rapids, Mich.: Baker Academic, 2003), 73.

2. "A Faith Revolution Is Redefining 'Church' According to New Study," *The Barna Update*, October 10, 2005, *www.barna.org/FlexPage.aspx?PageCMD=Print* (accessed October 10, 2005).

3. "Americans Draw Theological Beliefs from Diverse Points of View," The Barna Group, October 8, 2002, *www.barna.org/FlexPage.aspx?Page=BarnaUpdate&Barna UpdateID=122* (accessed June 28, 2005).

4. Thom S. Rainer, *High Expectations: The Remarkable Secret for Keeping People in Your Church* (Nashville: Broadman and Holman, 1999), 41.

5. Philip Yancey, *The Bible Jesus Read* (Grand Rapids, Mich.: Zondervan, 1999), 21.

6. Quoted in Julie-Allyson Ieron, "Spiritual Life," *Today's Christian Woman*, ChristianityToday.com., *www.christianitytoday.com/tcw/2005/004/11.54.html* (accessed March 10, 2006).

7. Annie Dillard, *Teaching a Stone to Talk* (New York: HarperCollins, 1988), 40–41.

8. Mathews, *Preaching That Speaks to Women*, 63.

CHAPTER 9: "PASTOR, PLEASE ALLOW ME TO MINISTER TO YOU AND YOUR FAMILY"

1. George Barna, "A Profile of Protestant Pastors in Anticipation of 'Pastor Appreciation Month,'" October 25, 2001, *www.barna.org/FlexPage.aspx?Page=BarnaUpdate& BarnaUpdateID=98* (accessed January 17, 2005).

2. Terry C. Muck, "Personal Prayer," ChristianityToday.com, *www.christianitytoday. com/bcl/areas/spiritualgrowth/articles/bci-030422.html* (accessed November 5, 2005).

3. Ellison Research, posted May 23, 2005, *www.ellisonresearch.com/ERPS%20II/ release_16_prayer.htm* (accessed March 2, 2006).

4. Ibid.

5. Ellison Research, "New Research Shows Pastors May Not Have a Realistic View of the Health of Their Own Family," July 19, 2005, *www.ellisonresearch.com/ERPS%20II/ release_17_family.htm* (accessed March 2, 2006).

6. Ibid.

7. Ibid.

8. Brennan Manning, *Ruthless Trust* (San Francisco: HarperSanFrancisco, 2000), 137.

CHAPTER 11: "PASTOR, WE HAVE SOME PROBLEMS IN OUR CHURCH"

1. Sarah Sumner, "The Mixed Gender Team," *Leadership*, Winter 2006, 89.

2. Ibid., 92.

3. Bill and Pam Farrel, *Men Are Like Waffles, Women Are Like Spaghetti* (Eugene, Ore.: Harvest House, 2001), 29.

4. Ibid., 18.

5. Linda Hartz Rump, "Is Christianity Oppressive to Women?" ChristianityToday. com, March 1, 2004 (accessed March 2, 2004).

6. *www.mayoclinicproceedings.com/inside.asp?AID=402&UID=* (accessed January 2006).

CHAPTER 12: "PASTOR, WHERE DO SINGLES FIT INTO OUR CHURCH?"

1. David B. Caruso, Associated Press, "Census: More Americans Living Alone, Especially in Manhattan," September 3, 2005, *www.detnews.com/2005/census/0509/26/censu–302456.htm* (accessed October 13, 2005).

2. Ibid.

3. "Bowling (and Living) Alone," *Wall Street Journal*, August 19, 2005, *www.opinion journal.com/forms/printThis.hyml?id=110007129* (accessed October 13, 2005).

4. "Unmarried America," *BusinessWeek* online, October 20, 2003, *www.business week.com/print/magazine/content/03_42/b3854001_mz001.htm?cha* (accessed October 13, 2005).

5. Jane Ganahl, "Playing the Non-nuclear Option," SFGate.com, September 18, 2005, *http://sfgate.com/cgi-bin/article.cgi?file=/c/a/2005/09/18/LVG9SEKU8C1.DTL* (accessed October 13, 2005).

6. Charles Colson, "The New Normal," *Breakpoint*, December 11, 2003, *www.pfm. org/AM/PrinterTemplate.cfm?Site=bp&Section=BreakPoint1&template* (accessed October 13, 2005).

7. Quoted in June Mathews, "Singles Ministry a Rewarding Challenge," *The Alabama Baptist*, September 8, 2005, 13.

CHAPTER 13: "PASTOR, SHOULD WOMEN BE CHURCH LEADERS?"

1. Sheri Adams, "Myth: Baptists Don't Believe in Women Pastors," *Christian Ethics Today*, Summer 2005, 23.

2. Terry C. Muck, "CT Classic: Can We Talk?" ChristianityToday.com, March 15, 2002 (article originally appeared in the July 16, 1990 issue), *www.christianitytoday.com/ct/2202/109/52.0.html*.

3. J. Lee Grady, *Twenty-Five Tough Questions about Women and the Church* (Lake Mary, Fla.: Charisma House, 2003), viii.

4. Ibid., ix.

5. Muck, "CT Classic: Can We Talk?"

CHAPTER 14: "PASTOR, PLEASE PUT ME TO WORK"

1. In *Seeds*, February 1983, 4.

2. Rick Warren, "Instrument of Blessing," *The Alabama Baptist*, January 19, 2006, 19.

We want to hear from you. Please send your comments about this book to us in care of zreview@zondervan.com. Thank you.

ZONDERVAN.com/
AUTHORTRACKER
follow your favorite authors